Straight Up!

A Teenager's Guide to Taking Charge of Your Life

Elizabeth Taylor-Gerdes, Ph.D.

Illustrations by Cortrell J. Harris

Lindsey Publishing, Inc.
117 W. Harrison St. #L220
Chicago, IL. 60605
Copyright © 1994
All Rights Reserved

Dedication

Straight Up is dedicated to your tomorrow, Julian-Sebastian, my little prince.

It is dedicated to stars on the horizon, Veronica, Russell, Rashida, Obadiah, Albade, Gregory Jr., and Nathanial.

Acknowledgments

Thank-you Donna Carter, president of Lindsey Publishing, for your vision and will to put *Straight Up* out there.

ISBN 1-885242-00-X

Contents

	Page
Foreword	i
How to Read This Book	ii
Introduction	1
Prologue: My Story	7

Chapter 1: **Point Blank** — 15
    The End Zone — 17
    Playing to Win — 18
    In the Spirit — 19
    Copping Out? — 20
    Lights, Cameras, Action! — 23

Chapter 2: **Rites of Passage** — 27
    The Legacy of Your African Ancestors — 27
    Lessons from Your Slave Ancestors — 29
    African-Americans Today — 30
    Your Rite of Passage — 31

Chapter 3: **Family** — 35
    A Family Is as a Family Does — 36
    Help Your Family to Help You — 37
    When Your Family Cannot Help You — 38
    What You Can Do — 38

Chapter 4: **Racism** — 43
    Just Another Man-Made Thing — 44
    Aliens and Earthlings - Trapped in a Lie — 45
    Staying Inside the House and
        Hiding From the Beast — 47
    Going Through the Door — 48
    What You Can Do — 49

Chapter 5:	Overcoming Personal Barriers:	
	Managing the Villain and the Hero Within	57
	The Villain Within	58
	The Hero Within	59
	You Choose	60
	What You Can Do	61

Chapter 6:	**Straight Up: Taking Charge of Your Life**	65
	Delaying Gratification	66
	The Wisdom of Applying Yourself	68
	Being Proactive	68
	Being Accountable	69
	Setting Goals	69
	What You Can Do	73

Chapter 7:	**Universal Laws to Live By**	87
	The Law of Cause and Effect	89
	The Law of Attraction	90
	The Law of Choice	92
	The Law of Guidance	93
	The Law of Abundance	94
	The Law of Love	95
	The Law of Self	97
	The Law of Learning and Growth	98
	The Law of Change	99
	The Law of Unity	101
	Conclusion	102
	(What You Can Do: A Quick Reference)	103
	About the Author	105

Foreword

Today's youth are greatly underestimated. They are a far different breed than the generations that precede them. Today's youth are more aware, intelligent, and inquiring. They, unlike their parents, demand new, stronger medicine for the problems they personally face and for the ills that abound in society. Much of youths' anger, confusion, and despair result from their disappointment at the legacy of divisiveness and spiritual drowsiness that is handed over to them. They have the capacity to grasp deep, profound truths - to look beyond that which is shallow and superficial. In fact, they want to do this. Theirs is a culture of boundless energy, light, creativity, and boldness. And where there is boldness there is magic. They have the magnificent potential to turn this thing around. And I believe they will.

How to Read This Book

There is something here for you. *Straight Up* is full of practical knowledge, ideas, and wisdom. Make it your encyclopedia for complete personal management in a dynamic world. Read *Straight Up* regularly, thoughtfully, and completely. Listen to it. Take your time. Digest it slowly. Share it with a parent, counselor, friend, or mentor. After reading *Straight Up* once, read it again. Keep it as a permanent part of your personal library. Dip into it now and then, for inspiration. Grow with it. *Straight Up's* message is real and relevant to your life today and tomorrow. It will never go out of style.

Introduction

I am a human being before I am a race, a religion, and an occupation.
Kris Parker a.k.a. KRS-One (1965-)

As an aware and intelligent teenager you may wonder as you look out at the world today. You may ask, "What's in store for me? What do I need and where do I go to get it?" You may ask, "What's the point?"

The point is that each life is unique and has three purposes.

1. You should enjoy life.
2. You have a responsibility to do your best.
3. You are here to help others.

But somehow, many people are missing the point.

The problems you face as a young African-American today are many - self-doubt, little support, racism and, perhaps poverty and a dysfunctional family environment. These things get in your way. They cloud your view and threaten your ability to fulfill your purpose. The conflict, hatred, shallowness, and confusion in the world around you are things you cannot control. They make you feel doubtful about your future. You might even be angry at what you see. You want to live your life. But you need answers, new ones. Where do you go? Where do you turn? Why not yourself? Why not turn to being human first?

You live in a society with many ills. People oppose and fight each other because they do not understand nor can they accept each other's differences. There is sexism, moral conflicts, and political strife. And African-Americans and whites seem to have a long way to go before racial conflicts are resolved.

In the African-American community there are many divisions. There are those who believe that the way to solve its problems is to go back to its African roots. There are those who believe that the community can heal its wounds by abandoning African-American culture and totally conforming to the culture of white America. There are those who choose to whine, blame, and see themselves as always being the victims - waiting for someone else to come to their rescue. And there are those who just cop out altogether. They create a counterculture of crime, drugs, fear, hopelessness, and self-destruction. None of these approaches has worked. None of them will ever work.

I think the problem is that many people get too caught up in their culture or gender and are too influenced by their experiences. This makes them see themselves and other people in a very limited way. They get caught up in who they think they are and who they think other people are. For example, many women get too caught up in feminism. They adopt radical feminist attitudes that limit their ability to grow. Whites are too caught up in being white, blacks are too caught up in being black, and so on. Many people allow only their religions to define who they are, how they should think and behave, and which groups of people they should like or dislike. These people are much too influenced by the past and do not look objectively at the present or future. They have a distorted view of themselves, others, and life. They are out of touch with the truth about human nature and the basic principles of life that bind everyone together. Therefore, they do not participate in life as full human beings. The future of America and the world demands that people get beyond these kinds of limitations.

Your culture and gender are like the clothes that cover a body. In this analogy your body represents your humanity. Your racial characteristics should make life interesting and enrich its quality. People were not meant to be divided because of their differences - but to do their own thing harmoniously. Like a pot of stew, all the different ingredients go into the pot to make the stew good. But each ingredient maintains its unique quality while being a part of the stew. Without all the unique ingredients the stew would not be a good one. The cook would know if a certain vegetable or spice was missing.

Overidentifying with culture and gender is like putting on a costume and becoming the character whom the costume represents. On Halloween you wear a costume of a character that you like. But just because you wear the costume does not mean you are that character. Underneath the costume you are you. It is the same with culture and gender. These traits do not totally define who you really are. And when you overidentify with the costume, you forget who you are. You are not being your true and complete self. You are not strong.

Of course, there is much to be gained from knowledge about cultural roots. African history teaches you that African-Americans are a nurturing, loving, and robust people. African-Americans are the true healers and without them, life on this planet would not be complete. You are to rejoice in this heritage and share it with the world while embracing other people's differences. Wrapping your entire life around this heritage alone is limiting. Especially if you do so out of anger and resentment at another race that you feel has wronged you. By only adopting an Afrocentric culture and rejecting other cultures you become the same thing that you despise. You are no better than those who have wronged you. More tragically, you limit your personal freedom to experience the richness life has to offer.

The truth is that you have many parts that define who you are. You are more than what you appear to be. And people who seem different to you are more than who they appear to be. You are defined by your personality, gender, ethnicity, experiences, and humanity. These are parts that make up your entire self. Your humanity is at the center of who you are. Before you were anything, you were human first.

And what do I mean by humanity? It is your essential nature. It is what you have in common with all other people. You feel, walk, talk, see, learn, and grow just like everybody else. And universal laws govern your life, as they do everyone's life regardless of race, gender, or other differences. They bind everyone together in this great experience called life. As a human being you have a universal bond with all other people - making you more similar to other people than different. Everyone is required to cooperate with universal laws if they wish to live a fulfilling life.

Universal laws are like an infinite invisible system that runs everyone's life, in the same way. There are certain rights and wrongs, and values and principles that are permanently in place and cannot be erased, negotiated with, or moved. They are a higher authority than race, culture, gender, or other differences. For example, some of these laws are well known.

These laws include the laws of gravity, electricity, nature, physics, math, aerodynamics, and many more. These laws govern the physical environment. The universal laws that govern people's lives are the laws of mind and spirit. These laws are like tools everyone can use to make their life whatever they want it to be. The wise and intelligent person recognizes the power of these laws and learns how to use them to his or her benefit.

It is a universal law that joy and abundance are your birthright. It is a universal law that when you show positive attitudes and actions you will find it easy to have the things you want, to get the support you need, and to achieve your goals.

Universal laws of mind and spirit are not mind-control or positive thinking gimmicks. They are the basic principles that operate in everyone's life daily - each second, minute, and hour. People do not learn about the laws of mind and spirit as much as they learn about the other laws. But they are just as real and important. Where universal laws of mind and spirit are concerned, there are no differences worth fighting about. There is only one truth - that all people are here to learn and grow. And they share their lives, talents, experiences, and resources in this process with one another.

Universal laws guide your life just as a river runs its course through a valley. The river's currents are strong, knowing, and steady. You can struggle against the currents but risk drowning if you do. Or you can swim with them and let them carry you. As you swim with the currents you can easily maneuver your way toward a desired destination. And because they are going in the same direction as you the currents yield their strength and support to you, and speed you along. This is exactly how universal laws function in your life. The laws help you reach your goals when you live in harmony with them. When you do not, you struggle and destroy your life.

Conflict, suffering, and defeat are yours when you fail to live as a full human being and when you go against universal laws. You stumble around in the dark.

Personal growth, joy, and strength come when you acknowledge all that you are - your culture, gender, experiences, and your humanity - and when you cooperate with universal laws. When you see yourself as a human being first, you can see how shallow arguments about differences really are. You are functioning at a higher level - in tune with the creative forces and laws operating in your life. You are free and strong. Your life is whole. And when your life is whole it is better for everyone.

You are the future. Your destiny depends on your ability to live as a total human being. Your attitude about yourself, your life, and your actions sets the tone for how society and the world will function years from now. Therefore, don't miss the point; flow with the river. Keep the following keys in mind on your journey. These keys are at the core of *Straight Up's* message.

1. Lighten up. Let go of negative, heavy attitudes and feelings such as anger, self-doubt, fear, and resentment. Let go of a past that does not serve you well.

2. Open up. Explore, take in the world and learn about others. Learn!

3. Give it up. Give the world and others the best you've got.

4. Live it up. Create the life you want by exercising your power of choice and working positively with universal laws.

Prologue: My Story

In order to help you understand where I am coming from, and why I think I can talk to you, I will tell you my story. Although my story is set in a different place in time some 30 years ago, it is not very different from the stories I believe many of you can tell today. Listen.

I was born and raised on the South Side of Chicago. I lived much of my young life in low-income housing projects and during the reign of the Blackstone Rangers, Disciples, and Cobras. These were notorious gangs that terrorized the inner-city neighborhoods. Their disputes were mostly around turf. Drugs and guns were not as rampant as they are today. But the stigma of isolation and the terror of poor blacks preying on poor blacks was the same. Peace and safety were not things I could take for granted.

I was harassed and chased home from school regularly by neighborhood hoodlums who wanted to do me nothing but harm. Even after I reached the building in which I lived, I was not safe. The hoods would shut down the elevators, making it necessary for me to walk up the 13 flights of stairs to my apartment. They would wait in the hard darkness of the stairwell for prey to rape, rob, or pulverize. I knew they were there and escaped many times.

I did not feel safe in or outside of my South Side neighborhood. Once when venturing into a white neighborhood with my younger brother, white boys, no more than 10 years old, flung rocks at us screaming "Niggers get out of our neighborhood." This was the first of many encounters I would have with racism.

Inside my apartment on the 13th floor I was not totally secure. As a child and young teen my basic needs were not always met. I went to bed hungry many times. I went to school in the fierce Chicago winters shivering beneath my thin clothes. Cold, gray, slushy snow seeped through holes in the bottoms of my shoes, which were already padded with tissue paper, numbing my feet. When my mother bought my brothers and me shoes and clothing with the little money she saved, it made my father furious. He tore them up or made my mother refund them. I will never forget the sad sight of my mother crouched and trembling against the wall as my father stomped angrily on a pile of brand new cheap clothes. Even though we desperately needed clothing, my father resented my mother showing her independence by secretly saving money and buying them.

When my father was home, which was very irregular, he often moped around the house. He rarely talked to my brothers and me or had a nice thing to say to or about us. He heaved a lot of hatred and anger on us - threatening and putting us down - constantly calling us ugly, stupid, no good, and burdensome. When he touched us it was usually to hit or push us out of his way. Sometimes he would just sit alone on the bed staring at nothing - totally cut off and unconcerned with us. My brothers and I usually stayed in our rooms and kept to ourselves when he was around. We found ways to laugh. My brothers were absolute clowns. They kept me in hysterics.

My parents' fights were nastier than the ones I saw on the streets - giving my brothers and me nervous ticks. We worried for our mother's safety. She was barely grown up herself - a child bride who married at 13 and had her first baby at 14. My father did not allow her to work outside the home or to venture too far from it. She was unable to protect my brothers and me from the stress of poverty, the ambiguity of being black, or from our father's powerful frustrations and insults. My older brother made it his job to watch out for our mother - often pulling my father off her during one of nightly their fist fights. We did not like having our father around. But it was only when he was around that we could get something to eat and decent clothes to wear. He made it clear that he was the only one who was going to earn and spend money on the family, and on his terms.

As I grew older I would understand my father's great suffering. He was an uneducated and unskilled man who had difficulty coping in American society. He was ruled by his anger and frustrations. He was not a bad person.

I was raped at gunpoint by a troubled war veteran who felt he had to use my body to prove he was still a man. I was sexually molested by a close family relative in my early childhood who feels no remorse about it to this day. "That's just the way it goes," was the unemotional response to me when I, as a grown woman, confronted that person.

Terror, suffering, hunger, neglect, abuse, and noise fill my memories of growing up on the South Side of Chicago. Death and fear for one's personal safety were a way of life. In the "projects" as we called them, smelly garbage, broken down refrigerators, and boiling-hot grits were thrown off the high-rise balconies with alarming frequency - sometimes barely missing people walking below, sometimes not. People just did things like this. Living in the projects had a way of bringing out the worst in people. And those incidents were hardly investigated. One took his or her chances whenever leaving or approaching the projects.

If my sleep was not disturbed by the my parents' fighting, it was certainly held in check by the riotous shouting, screaming, gangbanging, and police sirens in the streets below by bedroom window. Days were not different. I recall a hot June morning when sitting in my seventh-grade class at Forestville Elementary School. We heard a gun go off just outside the classroom window. I jumped up and scrambled outside with the other kids to the courtyard. There we saw a young man lying underneath the basketball hoop, twitching and dying in his own blood and urine. We stayed a little while, took it all in, and went back to class and quietly resumed our lesson. It was as though that young man's death was little news and hardly made a ripple in the low flow of life in the ghetto.

Life seemed to have little value in and around the projects. And it was very tempting for me to believe I had no value then as well. Among the dim memories of play and good times during my youth and teen years I had no heroes or heroines. I saw the outside world through the TV screen, which told me how wonderful it was to be white and how shameful and unlucky it was to be black. I did not see many images that told me something good, positive, or beautiful about myself. TV and society told me that "Blondes had more fun," and that I shouldn't <u>even</u> waste my time trying.

As a young teenager, hopelessness was my counsel. Solitude was my friend. My father told me over and over again that I was worthless and would never amount to anything. The white world told me I was just another dumb, ugly "nigger" who was not welcome as an equal in its society. The hoods and abusers told me I had no rights they should respect. The culture both within and outside the inner city urged me to believe that life for a kid like me was to be one of suffering, want, pain, shame, and rejection. Take it or leave it. So, I lived inside myself.

I saw many of my peers dropping out of school, getting pregnant, and going on welfare - forever. They seemed to do the only thing they thought was possible and acceptable for "ugly little black girls" living on the South Side of Chicago. I can understand how tempting an option that was for many.

All around me I saw the manifestations of hatred, selfishness, racism, irresponsibility, laziness, and loss of feeling. There was not a lot of love or support. There was not much enthusiasm to pursue full, rich lives. There were not many smiles. There was a lot about survival. It was cold. It was hectic, brutal, and scary. It was lonely.

Although I was surrounded by many negative forces as a teenager I realized I had a choice not to accept and give in to them. Things just didn't feel right to me. Therefore, I did not buy into the negative program that was offered to me. To accept things as they were - to accept what I was told about myself - seemed unnatural to me. The attitudes and lifestyles around me were not a part of the vision I wanted for myself. I chose to create an alternative vision. And it was from this choice that my life began.

I chose to question the life that went on around me. I questioned the quality of my family life and the quality of life in the neighborhood. As I questioned I began searching for answers and a deeper meaning. I wanted to know why I was alive. I wanted to know why some people were happy and why others were in pain. I wanted to know what was going on in the world outside my community - beyond the TV screen. I wanted to know my truth. My hunger for purpose was strong. I was like a sponge that opened itself up to the world to learn - to soak up all the answers to my questions.

I took myself to the neighborhood church to learn. I got a library card, checked out and read books about history, about life outside the ghetto, about philosophy, religion, personal growth, and spirituality. I sought out the elders in the community - engaging them to tell me their stories. And by opening up and searching, I got to know myself a lot better. My vision of my life expanded beyond the one presented to me by society, the community, my family experiences, the TV set, or the mirror. I began to feel right.

I learned that my life was not limited to the poverty and despair around me but that life was full of possibilities that were available to anyone. Through my searching and learning I connected not only with my African heritage but also with my spiritual nature. Both gave me a strong sense of completeness, value, power, and purpose. I learned that I was a unique person with a special ability to fulfill; that I could do anything I put my mind to. I learned that the world for a little black girl from the South Side of Chicago was not a hopeless, unfriendly place but that people were just their own worst enemies.

I began to value having goals and disciplined myself to achieve those goals. I learned how to distinguish the positive from the destructive forces around me and chose to be where I could learn and grow and feel good about myself and life. It wasn't easy because I am not perfect. But I held onto these values, embraced new ones, and have been guided by them to this day.

My father and mother eventually separated. She went on to get her GED and office skills training. She supported my brothers and me with her salaries as a laborer and office clerk. We all eventually moved out and away from the projects. After saving enough money from jobs I held at a McDonald's restaurant and the Prudential Insurance Company I left Chicago and began my life in

California - on my own. I was 18. During the next 20 years I worked while attending college, traveled extensively to other countries, and bore my child at the age of 38. Today, my work is devoted to helping those people who wish to grow.

As I look back I am aware that I took away many lessons and gifts from my teenage experience that enrich my life. The elders, church, and books taught me. The hoodlums, racists, and abusers were my teachers as well. But the most important gifts were from my family. From my mother I learned resourcefulness and self-sufficiency. My brothers gave me the gift of laughter. And from my father's suffering and failures I learned the value of preparing for life through education, training, and pursuing knowledge and wisdom. As I look back I am sure that I would not trade my background for any other. Believe me, if I could do it all over again, and be any race I wanted, have any parents I wanted, and live anywhere I wanted, I would do it all the same way. Because there are few experiences that could have given me such powerful challenges and motivation to grow in the way I was meant to grow. And I could not have belonged to a richer class of people.

I share my story with you because I am you. The problems you have, and the questions you raise now, were once my own. The answers and tools it took me much of my life to find can be yours today.

CHAPTER 1

POINT BLANK

point . blank (point blagnk) adj. {Orig. Unknown} 1. Aimed straight at a mark or target. Aimed at such close range that the projectile cannot miss. 2. Straightforward; plain; blunt.

(Websters II New Riverside University Dictionary, Copyright 1984)

The most worthwhile endeavor I have ever undertaken is responsibility for my own life. It's hard and it's worth it.

Levar Burton (1957-)

Once I get the ball you're at my mercy. There's nothing you can say or do about it. I own the ball, I own the game, I own the guy guarding me. I can actually play him like a puppet.

Michael Jordan (1963 -)

There are three kinds of people in the world. There are those on the field playing the game. There are those in the bleachers watching the game. And there are those in the parking lot wondering what is going on.

The End Zone
It's the last 30 seconds in the fourth quarter of the Superbowl. Your team is down by three points. There are no more time-outs for either team. Your quarterback has hurled the ball in your direction and the opponent's defensive linemen are gaining on you - fast. Clear ahead, about 25 yards, is the end zone. The crowd is on its feet, roaring.

Do you envision yourself sailing into the end zone or being rammed onto the tarmac by the heavy linemen? The dynamics of the world you live in today are just as compelling and intense. It's the final seconds in the championship game of life, and you can either score or get muscled off the field. The challenges you face are very different from those your parents knew. And these challenges require different coping skills if you want to get ahead. Like the running back, you must be adept, you must be alert, and you must be quick. The world is rich with opportunity. There are so many ways to make a living, more ways than existed 10 years ago. And the opportunities are increasing at an accelerating pace. Anything you think you can achieve is possible. You can live anywhere you want, pursue any career you want, and make as much money as you want. You can truly "have it your way." It is a fabulous time to be alive.

But this is also a time when you are under great pressure. Living a life of quality and abundance today requires commitment, hard work, good skills, and determination. What comes with today's opportunities are greater insecurity, fewer protections and guarantees, increased competition, and higher standards to meet - more than your parents faced as teenagers.

When more is expected of the average person, that person feels pressure. Having more choices to make on how you are going to live your life, what career you will pursue, what TV programs you will watch, what people you will select as friends, and what school you will attend is challenging and creates pressure. Having to compete with more people who want the same things out of life that you do creates pressure.

Because of the increased opportunity and pressure this is not a time to sit around and watch the world go by. You cannot afford to sit back and wait for someone else to come and make your life right, to give you something, or to even make you do something. This is not a time to squander your time and resources. To lay around and cop out puts you at risk of losing pace with the rest of the world and getting left behind.

It is much easier now to fall through the cracks. And once you fall through the cracks, it is more difficult today to get back on your feet. But you can always work your way back. It is never too late as long as you have faith, determination, wisdom, and resources.

The sooner you begin to plan your life, the greater the advantage you will have over others. Now is the time to prepare for your future.

Playing to Win

The times call upon you to dig deep and use all you have. There are as many ways to fail as there are to succeed. And this is a choice everyone must make. These are not times for excuses. The time for naming and blaming is over. No people - black, white, red, yellow, male, or female - can get very far by pointing a finger and blaming others for their failures or problems. You have many options. Your life is what you make it. Blaming, negativity, and idleness are not rewarded in today's teaming world; self-initiative, responsibility, and positive outlook are. Today people are less likely to feel sorry for someone who sits around feeling sorry for himself or herself. People are more willing to support you when you are ready to help yourself.

Playing to win means taking charge of your life. It is living according to a high standard - valuing all that you are and living with wisdom. It is maintaining a positive attitude and outlook, and developing your gifts, talents, and abilities - whatever they may be. It is making responsible choices and taking responsibility for the choices you make.

The thrill of a touchdown is shared by both the running back who achieved it and the crowd who cheered him on. In this same way playing to win is ultimately living a life that enriches both yourself and the human community.

In the Spirit
Everyone has a responsibility to themselves and to the human community. Nothing in life is totally separate. Everything is related. It is as though everyone is part of one great team working together to become the best they can be as individuals and as a civilization. And like a team what you do affects someone else in some positive or negative way. Think about that. Think about how everything you do from waking up in the morning to going to bed at night affects others. It could be as simple as smiling and saying hello to someone. That smile could make someone's day. It could be playing your music too loud and disturbing the neighbors. It could be driving a car carefully or recklessly to affect the safety of other drivers or behaving in a way that causes your parents joy or grief. It could be studying for a math test. Passing the math test helps you to pass the course. Passing the course could qualify you for science courses and higher training. Ultimately, you might become a scientist. And that certainly has some affect on others.

And because everything you do affects others, it makes you responsible for your actions. And because you are responsible for your actions you must always try to make sure that you apply yourself in the most productive way. This does not mean that you have to think about your behavior all the time. It means taking a positive point of view and thinking in the best interest of yourself and others. When you do this you will naturally act responsibly.

The world needs you. Its crises are not the sole responsibility of one particular race to solve. Nor are its triumphs the privilege of one particular group to celebrate. For example, environmental cleanup and preservation are not just "the white man's problem." And the fall of communism and the promise of peace between the Arabs and Israelis are landmarks of human growth all people share. You share in everything that happens in the world. You are a part of the human community, and you have a role to play.

You are who you are for a reason. And because you have a special part to play, there is nothing good or bad or shameful or inferior about who you are. The truth is that your life has a purpose, and your role is to live up to that purpose.

Copping Out?
As a young person of color growing up in America you, like many other young people, have a lot on your shoulders. You have more decisions to make on how you are going to live your life. But your major decision is to decide if you are going to play to win or cop out. This is an important decision. Here are two scenarios that place you at risk of deciding to cop out.

Scenario 1

The neighborhood in which you live may seem separate from the society around it. It might be a world that has its own codes of law and behavior. The rules may be to survive with the few tools you have. And often those tools may not seem like much.

Growing up in the inner city can be like living in a war zone. You may be isolated and surrounded by negative forces. You may be abused by parents who are preoccupied or do not appreciate you. You may have poor schooling. You may not have confidence in your talents or abilities. You may be pressured by your peers or terrorized by a drug culture and bloody and reckless gang warfare on a daily basis.

Outside your world you see diminishing government support, a complicated and intimidating workplace, and a low tolerance for people who are different. Your options seem to grow smaller and smaller. The life expectancy for young African-American males is low. They expect to die young. Young African-American girls see having babies and taking the welfare ticket as a safe way to go. School is not important. Schools and teachers seem to speak a language that you don't understand. They try to prepare you for a world that is more confusing.

It seems safe to stay inside the inner-city walls. It seems safe to have the baby, get the welfare check, pass the drugs, shoot the gun, and exist on the fringes of society.

Scenario 2
On the other hand, you may not experience these things. You may have a good family life, a wholesome community, good schools and friends, and never want for material things. You are, however, a person of color. And regardless of your social status you face a world that tells you that you are not safe, that you are inferior and unwelcome to participate as an equal. You feel that you must try twice as hard as others. Like many young people, you seem to be on the outside looking in. You wonder if there is a place for you because you are different. You look different, you act different, and you feel differently about things.

Many young people like you see life from these windows. They see it with resentment and anger. They don't see options for themselves. They ache from the heaviness of their dreams and lay them down. They are discouraged and don't even try to try. They throw away the rich and joyful life that is their birthright. They become laissez-faire - careless with their lives. They lose their self-respect and waste away. They drop out of life. And the ultimate cop out some take is suicide. This is not the way it is supposed to be.

Your life may seem confined to the neighborhoods that seem to represent the entire world for you. You may feel restricted to play only those roles expected of people of color. Or you may expect to have a difficult time just trying to get by in this world. I know you often feel alone with your problems - as if no one understands or can help you. I know the hopelessness you feel. I know the fear. I know the rage. I know it is hard. I know you feel you have been let down. But I ask you - after all is said and done - who is going to live for you?

Being born black is not a crime. It does not mean you have less value than others. It is not an excuse. It should not get in your way. Your blackness is your banner. It is a quality that you have and bring to the world. You owe it to yourself to be the best that you can be. Because you are the one who must ultimately live with your successes or your failures. This is your show - you are in charge of your life. Other people can only do so much to assist in your learning and development. But expecting politicians, parents, teachers, friends, counselors, or relatives to make things right is a waste of time. This is an all-time cop-out. At some point you must take the horse by the reigns. Hold on.

Your life is at stake. So you have work to do. Like the running back you must snatch the ball out of the air and fly with it - moving swiftly to a sound goal with grace and precision. Cool with purpose and force, the running back glides past the obstacles in his path. And you, like the running back, have the ball zooming in your direction in the game of life, right now.

Lights, Cameras, Action!
There are many resources available to help you move forward, such as free education, community development programs, mentor programs, libraries, good health, supportive friends and family, and much more. Of all the resources you have, however, the greatest is within you. Your life is governed by universal laws of mind and spirit that are undeniable. These laws operate in your life whether you are aware of them or not. You can make your life the joyful happening it was meant to be by recognizing and cooperating with these laws. Working with them gives you the power to control your life. Universal laws are creative forces that can bring goodness, well-being, and abundance into your life. These

laws are not bound by race, culture, gender, parentage, social status or age.

Like an umbilical cord attaches a fetus to its mother's body for nourishment, your mind and spirit connects you with the creative forces of these laws for wisdom, guidance, and growth. In essence, universal laws work directly through your thoughts, beliefs, and expectations.

The more you learn about your mind and spiritual nature, the more you will understand how these laws work, and the more you will beam into them. Here are the basics. What you think about most often you begin to believe. And what you truly believe and expect you eventually bring into reality. The creative forces of life will always respond to your deepest desires and expectations. Whether those desires or expectations are positive or counterproductive, they will be met.

According to universal laws, the most awesome power you have at your command is your power to control what you believe, think, and feel. And when you control these things you control your life.

Just as you steer a horse by handling the reigns, you make your life go in any direction you want through your thoughts, beliefs, and expectations. If you know what you want, and truly believe that you deserve it, and if you apply yourself wholeheartedly to achieve what you desire, then you will have the thing you want. If you don't know what you want then life will give you just anything. And just anything may not be what you want.

To work with universal laws you must:

1. Be aware of and accept your power to get the things you want out of life.

2. Believe that you deserve the things you want.

3. Wholeheartedly and positively apply yourself to bring these things to you.

When asked how they became successful many famous, accomplished, and wealthy people said that they knew what they wanted, believed they deserved it, and sacrificed and applied themselves to achieve it. You have this same power. And you have it because it comes with being human and having a basic spiritual nature.

CHAPTER 2

RITES OF PASSAGE

I am where I am because of the bridges that I crossed.
                              Oprah Winfrey (1954-)

Living with universal laws and wisdom is a legacy that your African and slave ancestors left to you. This is a legacy that is yours to carry on as your rite of passage from youth to adulthood begins.

The Legacy of Your African Ancestors
Your tribal mothers and fathers understood their power to control their lives. And they used it. They had close ties with the animals and the earth. They appreciated and respected the earth and all living things. To them, everything was connected and related to everything else. Each person, plant, animal, and thing had a role to play in the big picture of life.

Your African ancestors respected themselves and each other. Life was to be celebrated. They regarded the joy and pain of living as sacred. Because to them, life was a great journey and opportunity to learn and grow.

Your ancestors believed that each tribal member was responsible for directing his or her life. They believed that bad situations could be changed into good ones. They believed that the individual was largely responsible for his or her own misfortunes and that he or she also possessed the means to overcome those misfortunes.

Your ancestors believed that the causes of pain and suffering were the result of one's misdeeds. Successes and failures in life were attributed to personal initiative and destiny.

Your African ancestors taught self-love, respect, and responsibility. They taught how to love beyond yourself - to have compassion and reverence for all life including the strong and the weak. From your African ancestors you can learn to trust in your own humanity and that of others.

Lessons From Your Slave Ancestors
The beliefs of your African ancestors were passed down to your slave ancestors. Ancient beliefs helped your slave ancestors survive the challenges of slavery. Like the African ancestors, the slaves believed that life was a gift to all and a great journey that challenged one to learn and grow. Many slaves saw slavery as a test of their will to think as free and equal men and women. The slaves' culture bolstered their self-esteem, courage, and confidence, and served as a defense against spiritual degradation. In essence, their bodies were in chains but their minds and spirits were not. The spirit of the slave community was united and not solely dependent on the white culture that oppressed them. They believed what they chose to believe. They used group codes to communicate and protect themselves. They had their own values. This gave the slaves freedom from being psychologically controlled. Slaves could preserve their independence and resist seeing themselves in a negative light and being spiritually broken.

Because the slaves held on tightly to their spirituality the lives they lived as slaves were not lived in vain. They made the best of their lives despite their hardships, by staying on the moral high ground and keeping their integrity as individuals and as a people.

The slaves never lost belief in their inherent freedom and equality. This belief held them together. The slaves demonstrated how to survive through spiritual faith and unity.

African-Americans Today

African-Americans have always been a loving and compassionate people. Love was the basic rule of both the tribal and the slave communities. Love of self, love of community, and love of life were all included. African-Americans are a resourceful people. From your ancestors' close ties to the earth to the strong will and faith of the slaves, African-Americans survived by finding and using the many resources that were available to them. They are a people of deep faith and spiritually. They understand the creative forces that govern their lives. And despite the many challenges they have faced as a people, African-Americans have always believed in their basic freedom, worth, and the abundance and goodness of life.

Those who love and have faith and resources cannot be controlled. I am not talking about a meek, humble, and "walk-all-over-me" kind of love. I am talking about a love that says "I know who I am, I know what I want, and what I don't want." I am talking about a love that says "I love myself" and "I rejoice in life."

When you love yourself this way and combine it with faith and resources to achieve your goals you are acting responsibly. And when you act responsibly you cannot be controlled by the short-sightedness and limitations of others. You are not bound to the circumstances that surround you. You cannot be controlled by the weaknesses of parents. You cannot be derailed by the fear and ignorance of racist people. You cannot be controlled by friends who choose to sabotage their own lives by copping out.

Your Rite of Passage
Your rite of passage is the elegant legacy passed on to you by African and slave ancestors. Through rituals your ancestors learned how to turn their lives around - to make their lives strong and meaningful. Rituals were a regular way of life in early Africa. Through rites of passage, newborn infants became strong children, men and women became fathers and mothers, and children became adults.

Through story-telling, singing, dancing, and playing games, children and youths were taught the mysteries of life and the values of being responsible adults. The rites defined the youths' relationship to the community, to themselves, and to the world. Similar rituals were shared among the slave community. The slaves knew that the ravages of slavery would someday be gone and that their young people would inherit and master their own futures. Through rituals, slave elders passed their wisdom on to the young people - wisdom the young people would need and take with them as they moved into freedom.

Your rite of passage today means crossing that bridge from youth to responsible adulthood. You stand upon the shoulders of ancestors and other progressive African-Americans who built and crossed that bridge before you. You shed the innocence of youth and begin thinking and acting in a different way. As you cross that bridge you embrace universal wisdoms and new values - carrying on the tradition of your ancestors. The wisdom and values you adopt are like new clothes you wear as you outgrow old ones. They will comfort you and see you clear and safely through your journey - they will enrich it.

Rite of Passage

From Youth	To Adulthood
From Dependency	To Independence
From No Responsibility	To Total Responsibility

Rite of Passage Values

The Power to Choose
Choosing how you feel and act in any situation you confront.

Faith and Trust
Trusting yourself, life, and in the abundance of life.

Love and Compassion
Practicing love and compassion and bringing them back to you.

Self-Honor and Respect
Honoring and respecting yourself and bringing the same back to you.

Knowledge and Intelligence
Building your personal power by increasing your self-knowledge and lifelong learning.

Excellence and Meaningful Work
Commitment to becoming a better person by pursuing excellence and work that is intrinsically enriching to you.

Adaptability
Expecting change and moving with change. Making change your friend.

Responsibility
Taking command of your attitudes, choices, and behavior. Being accountable for them.

Good Judgment
Being guided by that which supports your growth and well-being.

Community
Contributing to the quality of life in both the African-American and human communities.

Integrity
Walking your talk. Doing what is basically right for yourself and others.

Grace and Objectivity
Thinking for yourself. Not bound by preconceived notions and limitations.

CHAPTER 3

FAMILY

I was barely 10 when our father died . . . Yet a member of our clan educated me and never expected any refund. According to our custom, I was his child and his responsibility. I have a lot of praise for this institution. . . it caters to all those who are descended from one ancestor and holds them together as one family.

Nelson Mandela (1918-)

The uneasy world of family life - where the greatest can fail and the humblest succeed.

Melvin Chapman (1928-)

Your family is your first relationship. You were born into it. Your parents can be your primary source for nurturing and support for your growth. They can <u>help</u> you grow to be the best that you can be. But being the best you can be is ultimately <u>your</u> responsibility.

A Family Is as a Family Does
A family is defined by its deeds, not necessarily by the people who make up the family. Your parents can be your biological mother and father or a relative or friend who acts as your legal guardian. Your family are the people who share your household and who may or may not share your ancestry. There is no special advantage to having both mother and father as one's guardians. Many

of the world's brightest stars came from single-parent homes or were adopted. And the worst public offenders grew up with both their natural mothers and fathers in the home.

What matters is the quality of love and support you get from your family unit, no matter who the people who make up that unit might be. And as you move out into the world your family will expand to include your closest friends, teachers, and mentors.

Helping Your Family to Help You

You are fortunate if you have one or two loving, caring parents who are there for you when you need them. But even then, they cannot and should not do all the work for you. Different parents have their own ways of showing support and caring for their children. When they do this, work with them. Help them to help you. Help is help, regardless of their generation. And you need all the support you can get today. You may not understand them or why they use the tactics they do. But try to appreciate the fact that they are there to help you. And to a great extent, you need them. Trust them. Tell them your stories, needs, and what you want out of life.

Give these parents support as best you can because they too are still growing and have a lot to learn from you. Your parents are dealing with the same pressures I talked about earlier. In fact, they feel these pressures more strongly than you. Try to understand their struggles and challenges. Because these same struggles and challenges may someday be your own. Try to learn from your parents' experiences. You can always find ways to make your parents' lives easier. When you do this, you are also helping yourself by helping your parents deal with their pressures. When they can deal with their pressures they are better able to respond to your needs.

When Your Family Cannot Help You
There are parents who mean well but do not have the ability or skills to nurture and support their children's growth needs. They can barely take care of themselves. There are also parents who are basically still children and have not grown up. They are unable to handle the pressures of life. Therefore, they become self-destructive and abusive. Many people have these kinds of parents.parents or other close relatives betray your trust by not acknowledging your needs for love, appreciation, recognition, and respect. How you were affected as a child, however, does not have to control you all your life. It does not have to destroy you. Parents who put you down or said you would never amount to anything were only projecting onto you their doubts and insecurities about themselves.

What You Can Do

1. Get to know yours truly. Whether your family life is jammin' or gives you the blues it may be time to begin validating yourself. Who are you? What do you like? What you don't like? What is your personal style? How do you feel most of the time? What makes you sad? Happy? Are you a shy or a social person? It may be time to start asking yourself these kinds of basic questions. By doing this you begin to learn to think for yourself and establish your independence. A supportive family should always be a resource for guidance and nurturing. But you are growing now and part of this growth is taking a good look at and understanding how "yours truly" functions. Sometimes deep problems and challenges in the family are signs that it is time to do this - to learn where family problems end and your life begins.

Getting to know yourself involves many things. It takes a lifetime. People are always changing and growing out of their old selves and into new ones. But there is something you can do as a rule to keep your pulse on who you are. Become intimately acquainted with what you think about most, what you believe about yourself, and what you expect from yourself. All you have to do is stop and listen to your mind, spirit, and heart.

2. Write your own scripts. Keep a positive attitude about yourself. Remember, abusive parents' attitudes and behaviors toward you do not tell the truth about who you are.

The truth about you is that you are responsible for yourself and how you are going to think and behave. Always strive to keep the most positive attitude about yourself. Learn to reject negative opinions about you that come from abusive people and create your own positive ones. Simply say to yourself "What that person thinks and says about me is not true. I am a worthwhile, attractive, and talented person." Chapter 6 talks more about this and how to improve your self-esteem.

3. Don't make your parents' problems your own. Don't take on your parents' burdens. Don't make excuses for yourself because you see weaknesses in your parents. For example, avoid feeling that you don't have to be responsible for yourself because your parents don't pay attention to you or because your parents display irresponsible habits. Avoid saying "I don't have to go to school today because my dad stayed out all night," or "I don't have to make good grades because my mom doesn't pay attention to what I do anyway."

The more you make your parents' problems your own, the more you will be bound and controlled by their problems. These problems will consume your life and prevent you from growing. And when you don't grow you only hurt yourself.

4. Try to understand. Try putting yourself into your parents' shoes to better understand their behavior and the choices they made. Try not to judge them as being right or wrong, but having made certain choices that resulted in counterproductive behaviors and experiences that affected you.

Try to understand where your parents are coming from. But do not make excuses for them. Maybe they have limited opportunities, weak personalities, or legitimate handicaps that hold them back. Maybe something happened in their life that broke them down - something they never recovered from. Maybe you are in a better position to help them than they are to help you. If you realize this and can help them, do so. But don't give in to the abuse; remain loyal to yourself.

5. Let go. Resentment is like taking a poison and expecting the other person to die. Try not to dwell on how wronged you were by abusive parents. You have more to lose than to gain by doing so. Don't rely on abusive people for support or apologies. It impedes your ability to control your life. This weakens you and gives people who abused you power to control you.

Realize that some people have not learned how to nurture or support others. Some people are not strong enough to both love themselves and others. It is easier for them to be negative and self-destructive than positive and nurturing. These people have a lot of growing to do.

Learn to recognize negative forces in your life and let go of them, even if they are parents, siblings, and relatives. Do not expect abusive people to nurture you. Learn to walk away from people who threaten your well-being and development. Wish them love and wish them growth. Don't carry the heavy burden of anger and resentment with you as you begin to embark on the path of personal growth. The burden can weigh you down.

6. Do what you have to do and move on. Don't be a prisoner of the past. No one can reach back in time and change what happened to hurt you. But you can decide how you are going to move on from here and make a life. When you find yourself in a highly abusive family situation that is not changing for the better, it is important that you move away from it.

This does not mean moving out of the house. Sometimes this is not practical. You may not be old enough to take care of yourself. Do what it takes to get by and survive in the present home environment until you are able to support yourself financially or find another more suitable environment. Keep this goal high in your mind. In the meantime do not provoke conflicts or give in to the abuse.

Letting go and moving on does not mean that you stop loving your parents and family. You should keep the love you feel for them in your heart. But loving someone does not mean that you allow them to hurt you or hold you back. You can learn to love from a distance if you must. Always keep your love in proper perspective to your need to grow.

7. Expand your playing field. Find strength and support where you can. Seek out relationships with people who will nurture you and support your growth. Surround yourself with these kinds of people and create an extended family. They may be relatives, friends, or school officials who can give you emotional or financial support or counseling. Reach out to someone you know and trust and ask for their help. Accept their help if it is offered to you. Make sure this is someone who feels good about you and is willing to support your growth and development. Parents are not the only ones who can love and support you.

8. Get jammin'. Focus on something worthwhile. You need a diversion, something to keep you from becoming consumed by a dysfunctional family environment, or just to help you establish your independence. You need something meaningful to look forward to. You need to make a life. As you maintain a strong, positive attitude about yourself, become less dependent on your family, and focus on your betterment, things will fall into place.

Get a hobby. Join a recreational group, club, or team. Work on a committee or task force. You can find about these things from schools or community organizations. These activities should be enjoyable and make you feel that you are achieving something and are a part of something worthwhile. This kind of involvement frees you from negativity and reduces its impact on your life. So can goals. Chapter 6 tells you how to set goals.

9. Find and treasure your family's gifts for you. You were born into a particular family for a reason. All family members have something to teach and give you. You learn from their experiences and examples. They give you tokens from family life that you will always keep with you. Try to look deep, through the pain and beyond the joy, and see what you are taking away with you. Treasure these gifts.

CHAPTER 4

RACISM

Sometimes, I feel discriminated against, but it does not make me angry. It merely astonishes me. How can anyone deny themselves the pleasure of my company.

Zora Neale Hurston (1902-1960)

Where I knocked, a door has opened. Wherever I have wandered, a path has appeared. I have been helped, supported, encouraged, and nurtured by people of all races, creeds, colors, and dreams.

Alice Walker (1944-)

Just Another Man-Made Thing
Racism is the notion held by some people that their own ethnic stock is superior to others. It is a primary belief that many people in the United States hold; some consciously, some subconsciously. And the people who hold this belief feel justified to hate and impose limitations on others whom they regard as inferior. Racism is both institutionalized and personal. Institutional racism means that America's social institutions are not set up to support the civil rights, nor the development and advancement of blacks, equal to whites. This includes the educational system, judicial and law enforcement systems, government, businesses, and so on. Personal racism includes the negative attitudes and behaviors that individuals of one race impose upon another. Both institutional and personal racism can be subtle or overt - quiet or loud.

Institutions are made up of people, which makes both institutional and personal racism a man-made thing. And like most man-made things it is flawed and cannot withstand the test of time. People do grow - some faster than others. And the good news is that there is less racism today than in your parents' generation. It continues to exist because both black and white people have yet to sort out their racial hang-ups and cast them the wind.

Aliens and Earthlings - Trapped in a Lie
No race is superior to another. Racism is a product of one race's fear of another race. People fear what they don't understand. Therefore, racism is ignorance, fear, and insecurity. Most science fiction movies, especially the old ones, provide a vivid picture of the way racism works. For example, usually, aliens from other worlds are immediately regarded with suspicion and stereotyped as being vile and unnatural. As soon as aliens arrive on earth, the earthlings scramble to get their weapons and annihilate the aliens. The earthlings do this without attempting to discover the aliens' purpose, or to understand and learn from them. Instead, the earthlings are threatened by the aliens' presence and intimidated by their "strangeness." The earthlings do not believe they can coexist with the aliens; the earthlings assume the aliens are dangerous, and that they have the divine right to destroy them.

This same attitude and behavior towards a group that is different is taking the easy way out. Because the more different a group is, the more effort one has to make to accept that group. Therefore, placing false labels on people who are very different and attempting to destroy them eliminates a lot of work. Indeed, this is taking foolishness to great heights. Because the real beast that must be hunted, cornered, and blown away is the racism within one's own heart.

One true evil of racism is that people who harbor it in their hearts and feel justified to discriminate, stereotype, and despise people of color are hurting themselves most of all. In the process of hating and rejecting the humanity of others, racists are sabotaging their own human and spiritual growth. They cannot be up unless someone else is down. They cannot see or get beyond their whiteness. Their whiteness becomes an ultimate experience for them, a prize and privilege from which they claim phony powers.

Racists are both hypnotized and blinded by their whiteness. They let it define who they are and how they feel, act, and live. This prevents them from living with integrity and according to high standards. People who are lost in their racists' attitudes lead superficial and shallow lives. They create a lot of pain and problems for themselves that they must confront and overcome. They trap themselves into a lie from which they must eventually dig themselves out.

Another true evil of racism is that many people of color subscribe both consciously and subconsciously, to the belief that they are inferior to white people. Therefore, the people of color set out to destroy themselves and their kind. These people behave in ways that show their self-contempt. They confirm the stereotypes that some white people hold, such as being lazy, not taking responsibility for their lives, not getting an education, or not pursuing a career.

They reject wholesome norms and values and adopt self-destructive activities such as doing drugs and committing crimes. They act stupid when they know better. They have no faith in their abilities simply because they are black. Therefore, they do not go forth into life.

Through their own behaviors many people of color help continue the cycle of racism, although their behaviors do not justify racism. Racism is a sickness and it is wrong, however, many people of color give in to racism and allow it to control them. Like the racists they are hypnotized and blinded by their blackness, and are not living with integrity and according to a higher standard. People who react to racism this way are also trapped in a lie.

Staying Inside the House and Hiding From the Beast
Racism is one of the biggest factors that prevents many young African-Americans from pursuing their goals. Like a menacing beast prowling outside the door of a house, racism stops many young people in their tracks. It intimidates them from venturing into the world to discover what is possible for them to achieve. They confine their lives to the short neighborhood blocks on which they live. They have no goals. They allow racism, the beast, to limit their ideas and their vision. They do not dare stretch themselves to know what it is to be truly human - truly alive. Symbolically, they stay inside the house.

Many young people see the beast lurking outside and feel ambushed - refusing to go out. They say "I haven't got a chance. I can't do anything without the white man's foot on my neck." I have heard this comment many times, often from grown-ups I know very well. They never let themselves go out of the house for fear that the beast will overtake them. Some even preferred death than going through the door.

Many young African-Americans experience the world from the outside looking in - from the television screen. And even here, the beast is ever present. It says to them, "You're not smart, you're not beautiful, you're not skilled. We don't want you out here, stay where you are." Or it says, "You can come out of the house, but only on my terms."

From inside the house and through the television screen the world might seem to be a place where the ones who enjoy life are white and the ones who suffer are not white. It may seem to be a place where the only people who are beautiful are white and the ugly ones are not white. White people might seem to be the only ones who worked hard, thought, invented, and created things to make the world go around while people of color sat around looking stupid. It may seem to be a place where only the white people have a right to feast at the abundant table of life while people of color scramble for handouts and leftovers.

These things will always seem true to you as long as you make racism an excuse for not living your life. They will be true to you if you fear the beast lurking outside your door.

Going Through the Door
When you go outside the house you will find that the beast is just a flimsy smoke screen. It has no substance. It has no life and no base in reality. You can go through and beyond the beast into the blazing sunlight.

When you go outside the house you will find that the sun also shines on you. You will find the wind also kisses your cheek. When you go outside the house you will find that people will smile at you as well. When you go through the door, other doors will open for you.

Going through the door means deciding not to fear or react to racism. It is deciding that you can be whatever you want to be, and the only real limitations to your growth are those you set yourself. When you go through the door you are not displaying the same ignorance and fear that those who practice racism display. You are showing courage, wisdom, and intelligence.

What You Can Do

1. Turn the anger into something else. Racism hurts because it doesn't make any sense. Yet it causes a lot of damage. Many people are still dizzy from the circle of hate between the races that has been spinning for centuries. Their visions are blurred, they wobble and trip over themselves. They are not clear, not focused. Get off the circle of anger. Shake yourself loose from the spell of hate. Be intelligent. Turn the anger into something else.

Much of the anger, hate, and rage felt by black people is turned upon themselves. They become racist to their own race. They moan and groan their lives away, drug out, gang-bang, rob, cheat, rape, and kill their own kind. Or they don't support other blacks, don't wish them well, or expect good things for blacks. They resent other blacks' good fortune and want to sabotage it.

To use your anger to destroy yourself or your people is giving in. You are playing into the hands of racism. You are making yourself no better than the racism you hate.

As long as you hate, you will always have something to hate. Realize that anger is a negative energy that can only produce negative results. It produces pain, frustration, fear, suffering, defeat, and more anger. The only thing that the anger will ultimately destroy is you. Let the anger stop with you. Use it for creative and vital purposes. Turn the anger into something that will promote the well-being of the race and human community - something that will lift you up, not pull you down. Turn it into determination and a fierce search for knowledge and wisdom. Turn it into compassion. Take your rage to a higher level. Turn it into a dream. Begin today.

2. Cherish and celebrate your race. Love black people - unconditionally! All of them! Those who are winning, cheer them on. Those who are not, wish them growth. Wish and expect the best for black people. At all costs, don't buy in to the negative stereotypes that haunt the African-American community. Conduct your own positive campaign for black people - the dark ones, the light ones, the rich and poor ones, the conservative and liberal ones, the strong and the weak ones. Support their businesses and affairs; buy their products; read their books. Help those who will let you help them. Love the race! This is not a difficult thing to do.

Learn to see the beauty and the good. Look for it. Show it off. Learn from its heroines and heroes; let them be your role models. Uphold its tastes, traditions, textures, colors, force, and beat. Celebrate its history, contributions, talent, and joys. Cherish its soul.

African-Americans are the original people. They give vitality to a world that would otherwise be rather dull. They are the conscience of the planet. Make your life a living tribute to the strength and grace of this people. The love you give your race will nourish and keep the community alive. This love will also keep you strong.

3. Don't hide from the beast. Throwing away your dreams because of the existence of racism is a cop-out. Racism is still widespread in U.S. society. But there have never been as many opportunities for anyone to succeed and achieve his or her goals as there are today. When you go outside the house you will find that support for your goals comes in many sizes, shapes, and complexions.

When you walk about in the world and conduct your life as a full human being, you will discover the many brilliant colors you have within you. You will become stronger. And in time, the racism that once appeared as a glaring, overwhelming obstacle becomes a mere, petty nuisance.

4. Mix it up! Racism is fear. And this fear is born of ignorance about people who are different. Show yourself to be a bigger person by appreciating the differences and lifestyles of other people in the human community. Include as your friends people of different races, backgrounds, and interests. Learn about them and learn from them. People grow through interactions with one another. Begin to appreciate the problems and needs everyone has in common as human beings. Once you do this you can see how insignificant and small-minded racism truly is. And the fear and ignorance of racists will not have any power over you.

5. Look before you leap. Choose to stick to your goals rather than react to racism. Sometimes your goals require you to deal with a person who may be racist. That person may be in a position to stifle your growth or support it. That person might be a school counselor or a job supervisor. Find out what people in a position higher than you want, and give it to them - as long as it is within reason. Always remember what is at stake, keep your perspective, and keep sight of your goals. You are moving on to something better. Think before acting. Try not to react to the person's racism in a way you will regret, but make your goals and reputation your priorities. Don't let another person's shortcomings hold you back.

6. Stay on your horse and ride. Your belief in yourself is stronger than any amount of racism. You will encounter racism in your journey. And no person or group can fight all your battles with it. This is your personal challenge. Racism will make you stumble and fall off your horse. You will have some setbacks and bad days. You will doubt yourself at times. But if you stay on the ground too long you are there alone. When racism knocks you off your horse, keep your focus and know that your goals are still waiting for you. Choose to believe in your abilities and goals more than you believe in racism. Don't dwell on the setbacks or the hurt. Don't make racism your god. Don't let it tell you what you can and cannot do. Just dust yourself off, adjust the saddle, and get back on your horse and ride.

When you believe in yourself you are embracing the truth. And the truth is always stronger than a lie. Your personal truth sets you free. When you believe in yourself you will be amazed at how resourceful you can be. You can make a way where it might have seemed impossible before. Your belief can create a groundswell of smiles, joy, and support from places you would not expect.

7. Educate yourself. Going through the door means placing value on education and taking advantage of the opportunities to get one. You can lose your job, your home, or your money, but education can never be taken away from you. Get some into your blood. Strive to get a college degree after getting a high school diploma, even if you plan to get a job. An education puts you on most anyone's level. Education should include knowledge about the world, a special vocation, and knowledge about people and yourself. Educating yourself is also making it a habit to question things. This is a true sign of intelligence.

8. Communicate effectively. The ability to communicate with various people is one of the most powerful tools you can possess. The first impression of yourself that you give to others is the way you communicate. And first impressions are hard to change. Interpersonal communication is a standard by which anyone's competence and intelligence is measured, regardless of race.

Learn to speak clearly, directly, and confidently. Make it a point to make yourself understood. Take pride in this. When communicating, show others that you understand their position without compromising your needs. Seek and enroll in public speaking, communication, and assertiveness courses where you can. Develop this ability by also reading, writing, and practicing your articulation skills. When you speak well you command respect.

Keep in mind that you are not being uncool or giving up your identity by practicing good communication skills - you are enhancing it.

9. Do the right thing - vote! Those people and groups who lack political and economic power are most oppressed by racism. Their interests and needs are not heard or represented where it really counts. Don't be among the people who sit around with their mouths poked out, complaining about the system while never bothering to cast a ballot. Government and politics are not perfect. But they won't improve unless people make them improve and respond to their needs. Your input is important. It counts. Participate in the decision-making process. If you are old enough, register and plan to vote in upcoming local, state, and federal elections. Take the time to become familiar with issues that affect your community and do the right thing when the time comes.

10. Dismiss other people's negative stuff. Understand that what others think about you has much to do with how they have been programmed to think. People's beliefs and attitudes may be unhealthy for you and limiting. Their attitudes reflect their problems and hang-ups and have little or nothing to do with you. Just as you would not eat anything someone hands to you, learn to be selective about what thoughts, beliefs, and attitudes you take on. Do not adopt other people's negative outlooks and attitudes about you. Make this a habit when dealing with racist and other counterproductive people.

11. Wish them growth. Remember that racist people also have to grow beyond their limitations. Those who are racist have their challenges too, perhaps greater than your own. Possibly their biggest hurdle is to overcome their own insecurity, fear, and ignorance. They have to confront their limitations and become something more than just being white. Don't take the fear, hate, ignorance, and insecurity of the racist person into your own heart. You have a strong advantage over racist people when you decide not to react to their problems.

12. Don't look for racism. Racism is an unnecessary evil. It is like smog in the air or pollutants in the water. People want clean water and air, but people contribute to contaminating them. People want peace in their lives but often do not know how to achieve it.

There are more nonracist than there are racist people in the world. Many people of other races want to know, understand, and support you. They want to be your friends. They may seem awkward around you because they don't know you. The little that they know about you is what they've read in newspapers and seen in movies or on television. They want to get beyond the limited stereotypes and may not know how.

Avoid being paranoid about racism. When you are you get more than your fair share of it. When you look for racism you see and encounter it everywhere. When you concentrate on racism it will find and come running to you.

CHAPTER 5

OVERCOMING PERSONAL BARRIERS: MANAGING THE VILLAIN AND THE HERO WITHIN

Each of us has two selves, and the great burden of life is to always try to keep that higher self in command. Don't let the lower self take over.
                                    Martin Luther King, Jr. (1929-1968)

The truth is that there is nothing noble about being superior to somebody else. The only real nobility is in being superior to your former self.
                                    Whitney Young (1921-1972)

You all have within you both the potential for greatness and the potential for utter evil, failure, and destruction. The true character of a person is measured by his or her ability to manage internal demons and allow for the fullest expression of his or her best self.

The Villain Within
With all the challenges young African-American people face, it is easy to understand how you could throw up your hands and say "Okay I give up. I won't even try." A strong and positive self-concept is sometimes a difficult thing to maintain. Evil and self-destruction easily set in when young people like you are most vulnerable.

Like the racist beast lurking outside the door you have your own villain inside your mind. Your mental villain terrorizes your dreams and aspirations. This is a melancholy, bad-tempered little gremlin who crusades about in your head cursing all that is positive and about growth. This gremlin speaks the language of doubt, shame, fear, anger, and ignorance.

The villain tells you that you are unworthy and have no personal value, that you have nothing to contribute to the world. It tells you that the negative things other people think and say about you are true. It tells you that you don't deserve to have your needs met or to have a good, healthy, and prosperous life. It tries to convince you that you are weak, that you are a victim of racism and other people's, abuse and therefore, you do not have to

take responsibility for yourself. This villain tells you that you cannot think for yourself and, therefore, you should allow your peers to think for you. This villain tells you how to hurt yourself and others around you, through drugs, crime, dependency, and idleness. It tells you to distrust people and new experiences. It tells you to be cynical and coldhearted, and to show an angry face to the world. It teaches you hate.

The villain within is on a mission to destroy you, to see you fail. It is your worst enemy. The villain must be stopped!

The Hero Within
Your public heroes are people who had the courage to make a good thing of their lives. Like the villain you also have that same hero within you. This is the side of yourself that believes in you and wants to help you realize your potential. It speaks the language of trust, kindness, purpose, and open-mindedness. The hero or heroine within tells you that you are special. It tells you that you are worthy of respect. It tells you that you have talents that

could benefit your community and society. The hero shows you how to respect your body and mind. It tells you to select as your friends those who will nurture and support you. The hero teaches you patience, wisdom, discipline, and confidence. The hero helps you stay on course and celebrate your rite of passage. The hero keeps you honest and true to yourself.

The hero's mission is to help you be your best and to enjoy the abundant life that is your birthright. The hero is your best friend. Nurture the hero within you.

You Choose
Whether you will follow the demands of the villain or the wisdom of the hero is up to you. Even when you are at your lowest moment, and when you are most challenged, you are never deprived of your power to choose which path to follow. This is something nothing or no one can take away from you. This is a choice that makes you constantly responsible for your behavior and for your own life.

Both traits - the villain and the hero - will always be with you. This is a simple fact of human nature. Everyone has a good and evil nature; however, the trait that you listen to and allow to guide you will be the trait that will dominate your life. The more you heed the bidding of the villain, the more nonproductive your life will be and the more negative your experiences will become. The more you follow the guidance of the hero, the richer your life and experiences will become. When you choose to follow the wisdom of the hero and heroine you must then decide how you are going to manage the villain within.

What You Can Do

1. Confront the villain within. You must search yourself and admit that you may carry around negative attitudes and beliefs about yourself, and about life in general, that will hold you back. Ask yourself, "What don't I like about myself? What kind of negative thoughts, beliefs, and attitudes do I entertain? Where did I get these thoughts and beliefs?" List the things about your personality that get you into trouble and that you feel you should change. Decide how you are going to change these things.

2. Embrace the hero and heroine within. Search yourself and acknowledge the positive attitudes and beliefs about yourself, and about life in general, that will support your growth. Ask yourself, "What do I like about myself? What kinds of positive thoughts, attitudes, and beliefs do I entertain? Why do I think and believe this?" List the things about your personality that help you and that you feel you can strengthen. Decide how you will build on your strengths.

3. Watch what you say to yourself. You talk to yourself more than you talk to anyone else. Think about that. What you say about yourself in your mind becomes true. Learn to monitor the conversations in your mind and the opinions you have about yourself. Learn to distinguish between what people think about you and what you think about yourself. This includes your friends, family, and authority figures.

Make it a habit to replace negative thoughts about yourself with positive ones. Quiet the villain and let the hero speak. For example, instead of saying "I'm so fat, I never do anything right, people don't like me, I'll fail if I try, I can't read well, I hate math," say "I am an attractive person, and people respect and appreciate me because I respect and appreciate myself. I am becoming successful. I approach my activities with confidence. I am in the process of improving my reading and math skills." The more you say positive things about yourself in your mind, the more these things will become true about you.

4. Don't be a toy. Victims are toys. They get played with. Choose not to be the victim. It is a bad habit. Feeling like a victim is a warm and easy thing to do. Choosing to feel like a victim is also a deadly trap. It takes away your personal power and makes you vulnerable to abuse.

Victims are those who have a habit of feeling that someone is always out to get them and take advantage of them. They are in the habit of feeling that they are controlled and abused by other people. They tend to feel that someone owes them something.

Victims would rather blame others for their own weaknesses and problems than to take responsibility for their choices and behaviors. People who blame others in this way are like children crying when they cannot have their way. This kind of behavior is for children, not teenagers and adults.

Victims have no power. Victims make themselves pawns in other people's games. Remember this. Whenever you feel tempted to feel like the victim, say to yourself instead "I am in control of my life. I am moving toward my goodness. I have many options and resources available to me. The difficulties I face are a temporary setback, and I am now in the process of overcoming them."

5. Adopt a mentor. Often other people see beauty, good, and potential within you that you don't see. They can help you bring it out. You can always benefit from the support of someone else in your journey to achieve your goals and become a better person. Open up to the advice and support of someone who really has your best interest in mind - someone you trust and someone who believes in you. This could be a family member, teacher, community leader, or a close friend. Two heads are always better than one. Ask that person to help you identify your talents, find resources, and set goals.

6. S-t-r-e-t-c-h yourself. Bust out of your routine if you find yourself in one. Plan ways to get out into the larger world around you. Try to go beyond the confines of your immediate neighborhood and circle of friends. Find out about city tours, field trips, or international youth exchange programs. Read books on various subjects to expand your perspective and understanding of the world. The more you learn about the world around you, the more you learn about yourself. And the more you learn about yourself, the less likely the villain can influence you with negative and limiting instructions.

When you take risks and stretch yourself your perspective expands. You gain a lot of ideas, common sense, and natural intelligence that are priceless. The world becomes a different place than it was through the eyes of a naive person. When you expand your perspective you can see more. You can appreciate all the opportunities that are available to you. You can see all the wonderful ways there are for you to be whatever you want to be. You are no longer a hostage of the villain, because you have a larger and richer pool of knowledge to draw from than you had before.

7. Listen to the music. It was the music - the song, the lyrics, and the beat that helped keep your ancestors strong. Most music is spiritual in nature - be it jazz, pop, rap, soul, classical, or reggae. Whatever the medium, music can uplift, inspire, and spur you onward. It speaks to your higher self. It charms you. Music echoes back to you the promises you've made to yourself. It keeps you in step with the rhythms of your ideals, amplifying your most important feelings.

Music is a release. It is good medicine and a friend. But there is both true and irresponsible music afoot. If you want to put a gag on the villain and free yourself from its downward counsel, and if you are truly serious about growing, you know which choices to make.

CHAPTER 6

STRAIGHT UP: TAKING CHARGE OF YOUR LIFE

I don't want to be the boss. I just want to be the accepted emperor.
                                    Harold Washington (1922-1987)

I made a commitment to completely cut out drinking and anything that might hamper me from getting my mind and body together. And the floodgates of goodness have opened upon me - spiritually and financially.
                                    Denzel Washington (1955-)

The things that get young people into trouble the most are negative peer pressure, lack of information, poor impulse control, failure to consider the consequences of their actions, and bad advice. These are traps. They are easy to fall into because young people seem to have so much leisure time to spend any way they want. Delinquency troubles and poor school performance often result from too much leisure time unwisely spent. Poor judgments can be made that create powerful obstacles such as pregnancy, criminal records, or personal injury, that permanently alter your life. When you lose your self-control you lose control of your life.

Delaying Gratification
One of the most common problems young people face is lack of self-control. You are young and most probably feel immortal. You have a young body, and perhaps good health, and your whole

life is ahead of you. It may seem that mistakes made now will have no consequence to your future life as an adult. Therefore, it is easy to feel that you should have whatever you want now, and can do whatever you want now. Many young people feel that what they do now has nothing to do with who they will become as adults. This is not the case. Everything you do now makes a permanent imprint on your life. Your attitude, decisions, behaviors, and experiences are now shaping who you will be as an adult. You take everything with you from your youth to your adulthood. Like moving from one house to another, you take all your possessions with you. Even though the new house may be larger than the old one, you furnish it with all the old furniture from the old house. You wear the same scars from youth on your adult body.

Today it is most important for young people like you to exercise self-control and good conscience. The world and this society are dynamic and demanding of everyone. Personal responsibility and achievement are the rule. No one can afford to do less than his or her personal best. Doing your personal best or not taking responsibility makes the difference between winning and losing in life.

Learning to delay your gratification is important. This does not mean that you do not enjoy life. It simply means making good judgments about what you do. It means involving yourself with friends and in activities and behaviors that support your growth and betterment. It is choosing self-improvement over immediate gratification of physical or egotistical needs. When you make this choice you may find that you have more fun, security, and freedom and fewer worries and fears. You can make a positive investment in your future while enjoying life in the present.

The Wisdom of Applying Yourself

As a human being you need to apply yourself in a way that nourishes your life and the lives of others. Work is the most common way that you do this. In many ways you are already involved in the world of work. Work is an activity that produces something of value for other people and contributes to self-sufficiency. The work you may be doing now might include: serving as president of a school class, singing in a choir, making your own clothes, fixing a car, or helping around the house.

Today, it is very important to begin planning your career and adult life early - to begin putting your building blocks into place. This way you can stay ahead of the increasing competition for jobs and utilize the resources that are now available to you. Work will be a very important part of your adult life. You should enjoy your life now but also plan for the future work you will do.

Being Proactive

Being proactive means making things happen rather than letting things happen to you. It is anticipating future needs and changes in your life and planning ways to address them. This requires initiative and taking responsibility. It is taking the long view and making plans that will benefit you in the present and in the future. It is creatively shaping your life.

For example, you may be graduating from high school in a year. What will you do then? Should you be researching and applying for colleges now or planning to take a job? If you plan to get a job, what kind of job will it be? What kind of preparation do you need? Do you want to travel and have an independent life before working or getting married? Should you research programs now that will allow you to travel? How much money will you need and how will you get it? And if you decide to travel, work, or go to college, is it a good idea to get pregnant now? These are proactive thoughts. You should plan your life realistically and carefully.

Being Accountable
Being accountable is knowing that your decisions and actions are generated by you. They are not determined by the conditions of your life. For example, your income level, race, or education has nothing to do with how you behave. You decide how you are going to behave. You decide to cut a class, do drugs, or join a gang because that is what you want to do. Your living condition, social status, low self-esteem, or racism has absolutely nothing to do with your decision to cut class, get pregnant, do drugs, or join a gang.

Setting Goals
Before a building can be constructed there must be a blueprint. A ship cannot sail to a desired destination without a navigational chart. In order to reach your goals you must have a plan. Most people who have achieved something in their lives worked with a plan. They succeeded because they prepared to take advantage of the opportunities that came their way. Your goals will change many times in your life; however, the basic approach to achieving them does not. Use the following steps when charting your course.

> **a. Set little goals to build successes in your life.** In the beginning give yourself little goals that you can easily reach - goals that do not make strong demands on your time and energy, but are satisfying to pursue. These initial goals should allow you to experiment and succeed at whatever you are attempting at the time. Be easy on your-

self. Reaching these little goals will make you feel like a winner. They will help you discover your talent, ability, and bliss. They will boost your confidence to think big and set larger goals.

b. Visualize larger goals. Be specific and think global. Create a picture in your mind of what your future looks like. Decide what you want and wish to become. What do you see? Focus on the clearest picture possible, putting in all the details you can. For example, what kind of work do you do? What does it yield? What kinds of people do you have around you? How do they treat you? What kind of clothes do you wear? What is your social status? Write it all down.

Think <u>BIG</u>! Think nontraditional. Don't limit yourself or think you cannot achieve something until you have explored it. Try something new. The world is in great need of new ideas and new ways of doing things. It has many problems to solve. There is a lot of work to do. You have the potential to help make the world a better place. It needs more scientists, environmentalists, statesmen, engineers, thinkers, and healers. Chart your own unique course. Seek the road less traveled. Avoid the crowds. Go for it!

1. Find out what you enjoy doing.

2. Decide if your goal is something you can or already do well.

3 Make sure it is realistic and you can see yourself achieving it.

4. Determine why you want to pursue the goal. Is it for money, fame, material goods, self-satisfaction, to help others, or something else? Be very clear about why you want to pursue a particular goal.

c. Develop an action plan. Read and talk to people; do research. Identify specific steps that you will take to achieve your goal. You will know this based on your research.

For example, do you have to go to college? Do you need a certain amount of money? Do you need to learn a new skill? Do you need a mentor? Do you need a certain job or position to prepare yourself? Will you have to adopt new habits or make new associations? Who do you need to call? Who do you need to know?

Put together a time frame or schedule. When do you want to achieve this goal? Work with a daily plan.

d. Execute your plan. Get moving. An idea is just an idea without the energy to give it momentum and reality. Once you determine what steps to take, just do it. You take one step forward and the creative forces that are always there to support your efforts will take two steps towards you. A house gets built one brick at a time. Taking each step in your action plan in turn, will help you achieve your goal.

e. Identify resources and support. Identify the resources available to you for support. There are school and community programs for youth; there are many nationwide programs that offer a variety of support services. You can learn about them through your school counselor. Determine what you need in order to develop your talents and abilities (training, internships, and so on).

Another important thing to do is to make sure you surround yourself with people who truly want you to do well and succeed. Let people help you.

f. Persevere and keep the faith. Don't give up when things get tough. Understand that you will naturally run into obstacles along the way. Don't be discouraged by them. Overcoming obstacles will only make you stronger and make the achievement of your goal more rewarding to you.

Never lose faith in yourself, in the humanity of others, or in the creative forces that are always there for you. Believe that you deserve to achieve your goals. Believe in the goodness of people and that they will help you. And above all, believe in yourself and your ability to achieve your goals.

In taking charge of your life you must first learn how to delay gratification, be proactive, be accountable, and set goals. But you are not totally in charge unless you also learn to control five critical things: your health, relationships, reputation, self-esteem, and attitude. These are the things you truly can control, to a large degree.

What You Can Do

1. Believe and invest in your magnificence. You have talents and abilities that are unique. You have a responsibility to yourself to fulfill your potential and honor the life that is yours. There is a stage in the theater of life that belongs exclusively to you. Only you can shine on that stage. Find that stage, go directly to it, claim it, and work it.

2. Broadcast your dreams. No one will know what you want to do or what you do well unless you broadcast it. This does not mean bragging. Nor is it to be confused with the idea that other people owe you something - they don't. Broadcasting your dreams is honoring your vision and talent and wanting to give them to the world. Seek out community leaders, school officials, or people who are already working in the field you want to pursue. Tell your stories to those who will listen. You already have resources and support that you may not know about. But you must make yourself visible before these things can gravitate to you.

3. Keep your vehicle in good condition. You can change many cars over a lifetime. But your physical body is the only vehicle you will have to carry you through your life's journey. How you care for it today will affect how it will function years from now.

The world today is full of unhealthy temptations - more than your parents knew. Many teenagers' lives are destroyed by drugs and AIDS. Or their growth is stunted because they must take care of babies before they can get a handle on themselves. These are choices they made. An intelligent person regards his and her body with great affection, practices common sense and moderation, and considers the consequences of any action taken involving his or her body.

Taking charge of your life means taking charge of your body. Try not to go to extremes where your desires are concerned. Respect your body. Watch what you put into it and what you do with it. Keep in mind that true manhood and womanhood does not come with biological maturity; it is earned by living a responsible life. And there are no better highs or pleasures than the ones you get when you are winning at life.

4. Take good care of your self-esteem. Next to your life, your self-esteem is your most precious possession. Your self-esteem is your measurement of personal worth. That measurement is whatever you want it to be. You can see yourself as being worth $5, billions of dollars, or priceless. You can see yourself as being worthy of respect and success or not. Your self-esteem is the way you feel about yourself and what you believe is possible for you. It is the range you set upon your own horizons. This basic belief determines what you will experience throughout your life.

Your self-esteem is like the engine of a car. It requires proper maintenance and care. A car will not run well on a poorly maintained engine. Likewise, your life will not run well if your self-esteem is poorly maintained - if the value you place on yourself is low.

Yes, you can control your self-esteem. You are doing it already - at this moment. Maintaining positive self-esteem includes all that is said in this book.

You can do a lot to control your frame of mind and attitude. To keep your self-esteem high you must get into the habit of feeding your mind positive thoughts and beliefs. Like healthy food nourishes the body, positive thoughts and beliefs nourish your self-esteem. Over time, the body that was fed healthy food shows vigor and vitality while the body that was fed unhealthy food shows illness, decay, and weakness. Your self-esteem works in this same way.

People wear their self-esteem on their faces. You can usually tell if someone has positive or poor self-esteem by looking into his or her face and eyes. Positive people tend to look lively, they seem to be on a logical and delightful mission, and you feel good around them. Negative people tend to carry a shadow. They tend to be troublesome and have many problems and worries. They exude a lack of confidence and doubt. They drain and bring you down. You can also determine a person's self-esteem by looking at the quality of his or her experiences.

These days it is challenging to keep positive self-esteem, because you constantly have negative thoughts, criticisms, images, and impressions thrown at you. But once you are in the habit of being positive about yourself, your potential, and life in general, it becomes easy. It becomes second nature. You can choose which beliefs you will accept and which you will not accept. It becomes as easy as sifting through a box of toys, removing those toys that are soiled and broken, and keeping those that are intact and in good condition.

When sifting though your box of beliefs, reject cynicism and feelings of worthlessness and victimization. Throw them away. Select beliefs that say you are worthwhile, special, talented, loving, likable, beautiful, in command, and in demand. Polish them up and preserve them. With time and practice you will become a pro at sifting though your box of beliefs and you will begin filling it with new ones of your own choosing. Now that you know that you control your self-esteem here are two key ways to do it. You can start today and now.

> **a. Replace those old mental tapes with new ones.** Everyone plays a mental program in their minds. Many people take for granted what they say to and about themselves on these tapes. Mental tapes are like the music that is played on a cassette or CD player, or the data on a computer disc. However, the information you hear on your mental tapes are your own thoughts and beliefs about your self, your potential, and about life. They can be very helpful or utterly destructive. Your thoughts and beliefs were programmed into your mind by your childhood experiences and by the messages and images you have absorbed over a long period of time. The thoughts and beliefs programmed on your tapes come from the media, television, friends, family, teachers, counselors, and so on.
>
> As a child you could not think for yourself and you took on other people's thoughts about you - namely, parents and relatives. These thoughts shaped the beliefs that you hold about yourself today. These beliefs were reinforced by society and your experiences growing up. Your parents and other people programmed you to feel either worthwhile or unworthy. They did this by putting you down - calling or treating you as if you were stupid and ugly, or by doing the opposite. They also did this by taking care of your needs or neglecting them. Your parents had a lot of power then to shape your beliefs. You have that same power today as an independently thinking person.

What thoughts and beliefs are you playing on your tape? What are you saying about life and how you view it? Many of you were programmed to view life and yourselves negatively. Here are some examples: "Oh, I'll never be able to do that. I wish I could be as talented as her. People don't like me because . . . " or "Life is a bitch."

You must begin to erase these tapes!

Pay attention to the thoughts and beliefs you are playing on these tapes. What you say over and over again in your mind comes true. In the same way you can erase and reprogram a cassette or computer disc, you can manage your beliefs. But you must first become aware of them. And when you hear negative thoughts and beliefs playing in your mind, catch them! And immediately replace them with new ones that say just the opposite. For example, when you catch yourself saying, "I will never be able to do that," say to yourself "That is not true. I am in the process of learning how to do that."

The more you catch those negative beliefs and replace them with new positive ones, the fainter the old program will become over time. This requires paying attention, discipline, and commitment. You must take yourself seriously. But be patient with yourself because those old tapes were not programmed overnight.

b. Learn to criticize your behavior not yourself. This may sound tricky. But there is a big different between criticizing your actions and yourself. A big difference. When you criticize yourself you are putting yourself down and negatively judging yourself. You must always try to give yourself the most positive feedback possible. Give yourself the benefit of a doubt. Because there will always be people, practically lining up, to criticize you. And you certainly don't need to be in that line. Period. When you criticizeyourself you are defeating your own purposes. You are running the risk of internalizing self-defeating beliefs. You are putting soiled and broken toys into your toy box.

It is easier to change your behavior than it is to change yourself. Criticizing only your behavior protects you, personally, from the criticism itself. You are not punishing yourself with negative feedback that you probably don't need. You are criticizing what you did, not who you are. It is the thing you did that was wrong, not you. When you criticize only your behavior you are free to decide however you want to behave in the future - which might be differently. You place less negative pressure on yourself.

For example, avoid saying "I am so stupid." Instead say "I did a stupid thing," or "That was a stupid thing to do." See the difference? Very subtle but very important. Here is another one. Instead of saying "I am so absentminded and foolish," say "That was an absentminded and foolish thing for me to do." Learn how to do this when you feel tempted to criticize other people as well. When you criticize others learn to criticize their behaviors instead of who they are. As you practice on other people you also get better at doing it on yourself.

Also watch how much you apologize for yourself. Overapologizing for yourself also means you have some negative beliefs to change.

    c. Stick to your beliefs. Once you have gotten into the habit of programming positive thoughts and beliefs onto your tapes, stick to them. Hold on to them at all costs - when times are easy or daring. The greater the adversity and challenge you face, the tighter you should hold on to them. Positive thoughts and beliefs are your lifeline. Don't let anyone talk you out of them. The tighter you hold onto them, the more they will change your life.

5. Put together a tight crew. When choosing friends, choose winners, not losers. And know the difference between the two. Make it a point to have friends and associates who do four things:

    1. They care for you.
    2. They share your values and key interests.
    3. They support your growth and development.
    4. They are progressive-minded and have goals.

People should meet these criteria before you adopt them as friends. There should be no exceptions. A bad crew will break your life down. These criteria make it easy to distinguish between your real friends and those who mean you no good.

6. Don't be a gloom-and-doom junkie. Research has found that on a regular basis a disproportionate number of African-American youth read materials and watch movies and TV programs that depict anger, terror, violence, and mayhem.

Psychologists state that this is because many African-American youths feel hopeless and powerless. Indulging in other people's suffering and pain gives comfort and makes them feel more secure, alive, and powerful, either consciously or subconsciously. However, this is not a good way to feel secure, alive, and powerful. It is short-lived and shallow. Other people's pain should not be a source of gratification.

Of course, I like intense, horror movies once in a while - to get my mind off things. I like to feel a little scared and mystified sometimes. It can be fun and entertaining. But overdosing on such negative messages is another matter. It is very unhealthy and it prevents you from developing and maintaining a positive mental attitude and outlook.

And check this. Bad news sells best. Or as the saying goes "No news is good news." Newspapers, TV, radio, and music inform people on what is going on; however, they are more often messengers of doom and gloom. The bombardment of bad news keeps people feeling helpless. Understand this. Sure it's real. But even here you can and must discriminate to control your mental climate. Try not to overdose on what is wrong and bad with the world. But search out what is good about it as well. Savor that.

Try to balance the kinds of images you take into your mind. Like your body, respect your mind. Don't overwhelm it with negative images and ideas. Seek out and expose yourself to images that celebrate love, beauty, life, and human kindness. Your behavior is influenced by your attitude and outlook. And your attitude and outlook are often shaped by the images you consistently take into your mind.

7. Consider the source of the advice you get. When people give you advice, grown-ups, persons of authority, or friends, always take a good look at their character. How do they live their lives? Do they make responsible decisions? How do their own examples hold up? Do they have your best interest at heart? Ask yourself these things before heeding their advice. And always make sure that the important decisions you make are your own.

8. Be a leader not a follower. Resist peer pressure at all costs. You may go along with friends, but make sure that you do this because you want to - even if the friends are well intentioned. Leaders make certain that their decisions are their own. Leaders may be part of a group but they do things because they want to not because the group tells them to do so. The leader's decisions and actions are also guided by wholesome values and principles. Whether you go along with the group or not, make sure that your decision to do either is your decision - not the group's decision. And make certain that it is a decision that will enrich you, not hinder you. True leaders know that they are the masters of their destinies. They lead themselves in the direction that best supports their growth.

9. Once more with emphasis: Resist BELIEVING You are A Victim. I cannot say enough about avoiding being a victim. That is one of the most powerful impediments to your growth. The real victims are those people who victimize themselves with their limited and negative beliefs, thoughts, and attitudes. When you tell yourself that you are a victim of someone else's behavior or a victim of circumstances, you give up your control and you give away your power to take charge of your life. You intensify the circumstances or strengthen people who you feel have victimized you. And when you do this, you make things worse for yourself.

10. Face out. Whether you are a shy or outgoing person, show the world your good face. In your journey pay attention to how you interact with the people you meet along the way. Unless they prove themselves unworthy, treat them with respect and friendliness. Everyone needs these things.

You don't always know what is on the other side of the faces you meet - who they know or what influences they have. Try not to burn bridges. Play your cards right. Learn how to solve problems, resist conflicts, and how to take and give feedback. Take people on their face value and try not to stereotype other young men and women or people of other races and backgrounds. This is not about being a square or wimp. It is about survival and investing in your success. Nothing can be placed into a closed fist. And it takes more facial muscles to make a frown than it does to make a smile. The more you show your good face to the world the more it opens up to you.

11. Pay your dues. There is a lot you must learn along the way while working toward your goals. There will be many people you must answer to. However, the time will come when you will be well established in your chosen field or vocation. You will no longer be the apprentice, you will be the expert. Then you will call the shots and will answer to few people or no one. But much training and learning must take place before then. Do the work necessary to reach your goal. Try to avoid taking an attitude that you are too good to do something, especially if it offers you a learning opportunity. Begin to regard all your learning and training as honorable work that supports your becoming a dynamic individual.

Dreams come true in their own natural time. They don't necessarily manifest when you think that you are ready, but usually after you have paved the way through preparation, hard work, and patience.

12. Grow through your problems. Problems and challenges are a natural part of life. You will never be able to avoid them. Your problems and challenges help you grow. That is why you have them. And the best you can expect is to get better at solving them. So instead of hoping that they will someday go away, you need to decide how you are going to handle them. Often problems and challenges allow you to discover and develop new strengths you may need in your journey through life.

For example, you may be challenged by having to juggle many responsibilities as a young person, such as school assignments and the demands of friends and parents. The situation might be telling you that your life is too busy, that you have filled it with too much activity, and that it is difficult to manage at this time. Your challenge might be to develop organizational skills and good judgment. You may have to learn how to set priorities based on what is important to you. You will need these organizational skills and good judgment as an adult.

In each situation where you face a challenge or problem, only you can understand what you must do to work through that situation. And you must usually do this alone.

The way to confront problems and challenges is to:

> **a. Accept them as opportunities to grow.** When confronted with a problem ask yourself: "What does this experience tell me about myself and my life? What is this experience teaching me? How can I grow from this experience?"
>
> **b. Pay attention to the silence.** You know what you need to do to get to your goal or to become a better person. Meeting a specific challenge is an investment in your growth. Learn to appreciate what is happening to you in the present moment as you meet the challenge. Are you becoming more sensitive, less rushed, less angry? Are you learning how to deal with fear and to take risks? Pay attention to what is happening to you while you are meeting your challenges.
>
> **c. Learn how to problem solve.** Don't run away from your problems. Like a yapping pitbull, they will only chase after you. Your problems have your name on them and will stick to you like glue until you work through them. The same kinds of problems will repeat themselves in your life until you learn how to confront them and do what the problems challenge you to do.

There are some situations in life that are tailor-made for you. There are problems that you must confront and work through in order to grow and stretch yourself. When you confront these situations head on, and with all the resources you have to bear, you come out feeling better. You fear problems and challenges less.

You may have either learned something about yourself or discovered something new. But in all cases the outcome of working through the problem or situation adds something to your life.

13. Take five. Learn how to be alone. Being surrounded by family, friends, and other people does not necessarily enhance you. It can often distract you from doing some of your most important work. Make it a priority and a habit to give yourself space to read a book, listen to music, watch a movie, go for a walk, think or meditate. Engage in any useful activity, as long as you do it alone.

Spending time alone with yourself can fortify you and replenish your life. You can get to know who you are and better understand your life - why it is the way it is, how you contribute to it through your thoughts and behavior, and what needs to be changed or maintained. You have much natural wisdom within you. When you turn down the volume of your life you are more likely to hear and be guided by it.

14. Think and act like an entrepreneur. Where getting a job and working are concerned, you need to consider this. There is no such thing as a stable, guaranteed job today. And often your best option can be to work for yourself. This can give you greater security and freedom than being an employee. But it also has its challenges. Being your own boss requires vision, discipline, planning, organization, and focus. It also requires a good personality and the ability to deal with many kinds of people. Being your own boss can be a lot more work than being an employee. But it's worth it. As you plan your goals think about how you can work for yourself. The business you pursue as an entrepreneur should be legal, productive, and offer something worthwhile to the community, society, or world. It should also be fun and make you feel good about yourself.

If you plan to work for a company, understand that you also need to think and act like an entrepreneur. This involves viewing your job as more than a way to get a paycheck. It means putting more of yourself into the job. It means seeing your job as an opportunity for you to develop certain talents and abilities. It means taking responsibility for your growth by choosing those jobs that will nourish you and allow you to grow as a human being.

15. Move! Activity creates momentum in your life. Find a hobby, join a community organization, or get a part-time job that does not interfere with school work. Volunteer! As you apply yourself doors and possibilities will open to you. By applying yourself you can discover what you do best and enjoy doing most.

CHAPTER 7

UNIVERSAL LAWS TO LIVE BY

*I wasn't concerned about the hardships,
because I always felt I was doing what I had to do,
what I wanted to do, and what I was destined to do.*
                              Katherine Dunham (1909-)

*Find the good. It's all around you.
Find it, showcase it, and you'll start believing it.*
                              Jesse Owens (1913-1980)

There are many specific universal laws that are vital to your life. These are laws your ancestors and elders fully embraced and lived by. They often referred to them as the "facts of life." Universal laws are no stranger to many in the human community. But it is always wise to remind yourself of their existence and simple truths. Their purpose is to help everyone experience the love, goodness, abundance, and creativity that is inherent in all life. These laws work with everyone equally. They are completely unprejudiced and cooperative. They are clear, precise, and always operating in your life whether you are aware of them or not. Just as naturally and predictably as the sun rises and sets, universal laws operate in your life.

The suggestions for growth and life enhancement described in this book are based on the laws of mind and spirit that are most important to you. Each law plays a distinct role in your life. However, they are closely related to one another. You can easily study and understand them.

Just as you study the laws of math, physics, gravity, and nature you must also study the universal laws of mind and spirit. See and understand how they operate in your own and other people's lives. Learn to work with them. Learn to live by them. This stuff is real.

The Law of Cause and Effect
Life is very simple - what you put into it, you get back. Every action you take is like a debt you create. There are good debts and bad ones. Every debt you make will come back to you. Good deeds bring about good deeds, bad deeds bring about bad ones. You may have often heard the following proverbs: "What goes around comes around." "You will reap what you sow." "Treat others as you would have them treat you." or "If you live by the sword you will die by the sword." These proverbs are based on this law of cause and effect. You must always be careful of what you put into the world, in thought, feeling, and deed. Because it always comes back to you. Like putting water into a well, you must some day drink from it. Therefore, you must be careful of the kind of water you put into that well and how you take care of that water. This is a fundamental fact of life. You must be careful with the way you treat life.

When you give your best to others and the world, you will experience the best that people and the world have to offer. When you give your worst self to others and the world, you will experience the worst that people and life have to offer. If you steal something from someone today, something will be stolen from you. If you help someone in need today, you will be helped someday when you are in need. It's just that simple.

The Law of Attraction

"Thought is a living thing." My grandmother often said this. Your thoughts, beliefs, and expectations are like powerful magnets that attract situations that match and agree with them. This makes the law of attraction the most important universal law.

This law works with you every day, hour, minute, second, and microsecond. Like a puppy anxious to please, waiting for you to throw a ball so that it can run and fetch it, this law works similarly with you. It is always there at your beck and call, waiting for you to give it a thought or belief to fulfill. You have got to be careful with what you throw out.

The law will always make the picture in your mind come true, whether it is a rosy picture or a sad one.

>**a. How thoughts work.** A thought is a loose idea. Thoughts come and go. You accept other people's thoughts. You give them away. You exchange thoughts. Here is an example of some thoughts: "I knew I would blow it. People don't take me very seriously. There is never enough to go around for me to have my share. I do stupid things. I am ugly." or "I am a nice person. I knew I could do that. I'm good, damn good." Thoughts that you entertain over a long period of time eventually become beliefs, like a sauce that hardens and becomes stuck to a plate. Thoughts become part of your personality.
>
>**b. How beliefs work.** Beliefs are convictions you have about something. Beliefs are thoughts that have become concrete. Beliefs are not as easy to change as thoughts.

They are imprinted in your mind. Your beliefs about yourself fall into two basic categories: (1) You believe you have value and worth as a person and deserve to win in life; or (2) You believe you have no value and no worth and deserve to fail in life.

Beliefs are your private truths about yourself, your potential, your race, and life. Beliefs are silent. But they become so much a part of you that you are hardly aware of them. You take them for granted. They become invisible. But they have a lot of power. Like your heartbeat and other internal bodily functions, you are not aware of them, yet they are running your body. Beliefs run your life.

What you believe deeply comes true. Your beliefs direct your behavior. They are your programmed instructions on how you conduct your life. You always act out the program playing in your mind and in your heart. And together your beliefs and actions determine the kinds of experiences you have. If you believe you are unworthy and a victim you will act like a victim. When you act like a victim you will always be victimized. If you believe you are stupid, bad, and not worthy of respect you will behave in such a way that people will see you as stupid, bad, and not worthy of their respect.

According to the law of attraction you control what you think and believe. And that makes you responsible for most of the things that happen to you - the good and the bad. Parents, friends, teachers, and other people cannot control how you think, feel, or behave. You always have control over that. There is no way around this.

The universe is very cooperative. It naturally responds to your deepest feelings and desires by helping you achieve whatever you feel you truly deserve - whether it is positive or negative. If you feel unworthy and hate yourself, the creative forces of life will provide you with the means to self-destruct. If you truly believe you are worthy and deserve to express your talent, these forces will provide you with the means to do so.

Therefore, to work positively and cooperatively with this law you must become intimately acquainted with your thoughts and beliefs about yourself, your potential, your race, and your life. If you find that they do not serve you well, change them. Immediately. A movie director who is not pleased with a script, says "Cut. Change that phrase. It doesn't sound right." You have the same power to alter your experiences. Just as hardened sauce on a plate can be scraped away, you can remove self-defeating thoughts and beliefs and replace them with positive and nurturing ones.

Also, expect the best. Aim high. Expect to become better and better. Expect to have the things you want - to have your needs met. Expect good health, nurturing relationships, beauty, fun, achievement, and meaning in your life. Also, learn to expect the same for others.

The Law of Choice
You always choose how you are going to think, feel, and behave. The most primary ability in life is your power to make choices. A person chooses to feel angry when someone insults him or her. No one can make another person angry, only that person can choose to be angry. A person chooses to feel ashamed when other people treat him or her as an unequal. A person chooses not to

realize that those who treat others unfairly are acting out of fear and ignorance. A person chooses to cop an attitude, cut a class, join a gang, or abuse someone else's property when he or she does not get what was wanted. All these things are choices people make.

The beauty of life is that you have many choices that you can make. They are unlimited. And during the course of a single day you make hundreds of choices. And they all belong to you and you alone. What immense power you have over your life.

So you can choose to like yourself. You can choose to see your life as a joyful happening. You can choose to see the many opportunities for you to grow and develop your potential in the challenges you face. You can choose to see your life as a brilliant picture that you paint. The colors you use to paint this picture are your thoughts, beliefs, expectations, and choices. You can choose to believe in your potential to achieve whatever you set your mind to. And nothing anyone says, thinks, or does can stop you. Only you can stop you. And you do this by choosing to doubt yourself, your worth, and what is possible for you.

Therefore, keep in mind that no one chooses for you. Your thoughts, beliefs, feelings, and actions are entirely your own. Take total responsibility for them and take good care of them.

The Law of Guidance
When you sincerely seek to grow and achieve something, you will always have guidance to help you. The earnest seeker is never alone. Guidance comes to you in many forms. It can be a creative insight or inspiration that comes from within you. It can be a strong feeling to go in a given direction - to read a certain book or take a certain class. Guidance also comes through other people

who may come into your life to support you. Guidance can come from a stranger who tells you or gives you something that you just happen to need at that time. Doors of opportunity and resources open where you may not expect them to. The law of guidance always gives you what you need to become a better person.

To work with this law you must first earnestly seek to be creative and constructive. Second, use all the talents and resources you have in the present moment. Third, trust that your needs will be met and your questions will be answered. Fourth, be consistent, persistent, and open in your search.

The Law of Abundance
Life is abundant. Life always accepts you as you are, whether you are black, white, rich, poor, able, or disabled. It gives you what you believe you deserve no matter what your circumstances may be. The creative forces of life exist to help you achieve what you believe is possible for you to achieve. This is because everything that lives must grow, whether it is a tree, a flower, an animal, or even a cell. The will to grow and flourish is inherent in all life. And there is always support in the world for your growth in whatever direction you choose.

When you take one step forward the universe takes two steps toward you to help you. The key to growth and having abundance is using what you already have. Make the most of what you have right now. If you are an artist, then draw, and draw now. If you are a singer, then sing, and sing now. If you see yourself becoming a scientist one day, then study science courses, and study them now. Do the things now that you can do to work toward your goal. Don't wait or procrastinate. The law of abundance builds on what you already have and what you are already doing.
Do not think that someday when you are all grown up things will

magically fall into place. There is nothing magical about being an adult that makes things work themselves out. The important work must begin with what you have now as a young person. Begin putting things into place now by putting your current talents and skills to work now. And when you do this, and expect abundance, you generate all the support you need.

The key to making the principle of abundance work for you is faith. This means believing in yourself, believing in your talent and potential, and believing in the abundance of life. Trust that the support you need is always there as long as you apply yourself. Trust that there is always enough support for your goals. Knowing that abundance is your birthright and expecting it with all your might.

The Law of Love
Love, compassion, and giving are the fuel of life. Have you ever heard the saying "You get a lot farther with a little bit of honey?" Or the song that goes "When you laugh the world laughs with you and when you cry you cry alone?" These sayings are based on this simple fact of life.

The world is responsive to a smile and a good nature. Love, compassion, and kindness are basic human needs. They are like food, air, water, and rest. Few people, if any, can survive without them. That is why love and compassion are always welcome and people will always respond favorably to them. And when you can make love, compassion, and kindness a basic part of your attitude, you will experience a more satisfying life.

Being loving and compassionate does mean being weak. That is one of the greatest misunderstandings. To the contrary, love and compassion are strengths. They make you strong because they make it difficult for people to control you and because they have the power to bring you the support you need. They keep your life on a positive note. This gets back to the first universal law - what you put out you get back. So if you want love, compassion, and kindness you must give them.

On the other hand, resentment, cynicism, guilt, fear, anger, blame, and hate are your real enemies. These things poison your life. They stunt your growth, affect your health, and make you ill. They are the major causes of human conflict and failure. These feelings attract negative forces into your life. They close doors where they should be open. They bring you people who will abuse you, disrespect you, or reject you. They make you idle and self-destructive. They make you hate yourself and others. They are like a ball and chain around your ankle that prevent you from running that touchdown drive. Once these feelings become a regular part of your personality it is very difficult to change and shake them loose. When you exhibit these attitudes you struggle and flow against the smooth currents of the river of life.

You can control how much love and hate enters your life. You control the quality of your life by allowing love or hate to come from you and to you. As a young person who has your life ahead, you - most of all - must learn how to manage your feelings. Do your best to avoid feeling things like anger, resentment, hate, and blame for too long. Manage your life so that there is more love, compassion, and giving in it. Try to maintain a loving and compassionate attitude toward yourself, others, and life, and fill your life with others who share this attitude with you.

The Law of Self
All life has a purpose. All that exists has a reason for being here. This is because all life is connected. Everything has a purpose to fulfill from the smallest insect to the largest animal. Everything plays its part to make this planet a place where everyone and everything can be nurtured, can experience joy, and can be challenged and grow. Insects help cultivate soil for agriculture, flowers produce visual and fragrant delights, a sunrise inspires, and a puppy amuses. As a human being you have something unique about you. And you contribute your uniqueness to the world.

You are special, and if you have not discovered your unique potential, it is there waiting to be discovered. It is there waiting for you to give it to the world. You have a special purpose for being here. No matter who you are or where you come from.

You discover your talents by getting to know yourself and by taking the time to listen to your heart. What does it tell you? What delights you? Get to know what you enjoy doing and what makes you feel worthwhile. How do you express yourself best? Once you discover your uniqueness, you can make the responsible choice to apply yourself positively to develop it.

You must trust yourself to stretch and take risks using what you have. Set goals that are interesting enough to keep you occupied, but not overtaxing. Stick to them long enough for them to come to fruition. When you make the choice to develop your uniqueness, remember that life will never give you anything you cannot handle.

The Law of Learning and Growth

Life is a journey where lessons must be learned along the way. Everyone must pay some dues. And it is more important to pay attention to what is happening to you now than to live too much in the future.

There seems to be too many things in your life that you cannot control, such as the behavior of family members, educators, and friends, racism, and the government. There seems to be so much injustice and ugliness around you. Yet the real truth is that you do have some control. No matter who you are, who your parents are, or where you live or go to school, you are exactly where you are supposed to be. Your lifestyle gives you certain challenges that you must meet and overcome.

For example, dealing with negative people who put you down may be a test for you to learn how to assert yourself and make your own choices. Growing up in a drug-infested environment could be a test of your will to love and respect yourself. It could also be teaching you something about human will and weaknesses. The racist insults and injustices you see and experience can be tests of your ability to manage your own anger and rage. And remember, individuals who are prejudiced are also challenged to rise above their ignorance and fear. Everyone is here to learn and grow.

My young lifestyle growing up on the South Side ghettos of Chicago taught me some valuable lessons. I developed a keen instinct to survive. By this I mean I developed an ability to be resourceful. I learned a lot about human nature. I came out of that experience with an ability to appreciate things that most other people take for granted. I know what it is like to go without the basic things a person needs to survive - food, clothing, shelter, safety, and affection. Therefore, I can fully appreciate the value of having my needs met as an adult. I know the importance of helping people and the power of living by universal spiritual principles - the kinds I am sharing with you in this book. Ultimately, I can say I am not naive about life. I can survive under most any circumstance. And I am still learning.

Your lifestyle may have challenges and lessons for you that are similar to mine. And perhaps only the life you have now can teach you certain things that you need to learn in order to grow as a productive human being. Remember that you are growing so that you can develop your uniqueness and give it to the world. Your character, abilities, and will are forged from your trials and hardships. All the problems, challenges, and experiences you have and will continue to have is territory that you must traverse before achieving your ultimate goal and betterment.

The key to learning and growing is to understand and appreciate the growth lessons that your life holds for you. No particular lifestyle is better than another. Rich or poor, able or disabled, only the challenges involved in each lifestyle are different. Lifestyles are like shoes. You cannot wear a new pair of shoes until you have walked about in and outgrown the old ones. Likewise, you must weather the challenges and learn the lessons from your current experience before transcending it and moving onto another lifestyle, perhaps a more desirable one. Try not to place any value on the lifestyle you lead; try not to judge it. Only try to learn from it. Try to find out what it is teaching you.

The Law of Change
Things change. Life is dynamic. The young turn old. Seasons change. People change. Change is necessary for growth. Without change, growth is impossible. It seems as if once you become set-

tled and comfortable in a situation something happens to upset the status quo. At first an unexpected change is upsetting and threatening. It challenges you to do something different. But eventually, when you choose to surrender and cooperate with the change, you find yourself settling into a new mode that is often more satisfying than the old one. That is the beauty of change. It gives you an opportunity to grow and improve the quality of your life - if you allow it to do so. For example, a person may have been working at a particular job for many years and all of a sudden the job is lost. The person gets laid off. That person can take the change as an opportunity to grow or can choose to resist the change by clinging to blame and wanting the old way back. This is not always an easy decision to make.

That laid-off worker may now have to learn some new skills that may get him or her a job that not only pays more money but also one that he or she enjoys doing much better. The person may even discover new interest and talents in the process. Ultimately, the person's quality of life is improved greatly by adapting to the change.

Change is like the wind that blows through the trees, pulling the dead leaves off the limbs and making space for new ones to grow. The tree grows stronger by having more new healthy leaves to absorb the sunlight.

When life sees that you are not growing it will bring about a change to bust you out of your routine and make you participate more fully in life. Because this is how you are supposed to live - fully. Change shakes things up and makes you participate and strive to live up to your best potential. And those who resist change suffer.

Learn to accept change and not work against it. Learn to make it your friend. Be flexible and adaptable. Move with change. Trust it.

The Law of Unity
Everything is related. There is a natural relationship between the things in life, whether it be people, actions, or experiences. All things in life are here to nourish and support everything else in this great experience. A single person's suffering or joy eventually affects everyone in the world on some level. Therefore, everyone is, in a real sense, their brother's keeper.

You need connections in order to reach your goal. You cannot reach them without other people. The steps and connections you make along the way are like pieces of a puzzle being put into place. The picture is not complete unless all the pieces are laid down. You may not know where a particular step will lead you, but taking that step is important if you want to make it to your goal.

People share this planet to benefit from the growth and contributions of one another. The more you become a part of the world and contribute to the well-being of others and life on the planet, the more you enhance your own life. Pieces fall into place. Your personal development depends on how you relate not only to yourself but also to the world. The more you open up and expand your world, the more possibilities and opportunities will come your way. The more you connect your personal goals to a larger purpose in the world, the more meaning you will bring into your life and the richer this experience becomes for you. This happens only because your relationship to the world is just as important as your relationship to yourself.

Therefore, learn to stretch yourself beyond your immediate environment or vision. Make it a point when you plan a goal to see how it relates to a larger picture. Set goals that not only enhance yourself but also benefit others. This could pertain to the community, health, environment, social issues, government, business, or world affairs. There is always a way to both enrich yourself and to improve the quality of life on this planet through your goals and endeavors.

Conclusion

Your life is your most precious possession. You live in a world that is full of possibility and support for you. You have the tools you need at your disposal right now to begin making your life whatever you want it to be. Your biggest obstacles are not the system, the neighborhood, lack of money, your skin color, abusive people, nor childhood wounds. Your biggest obstacles are the kinds of thoughts, beliefs, and expectations you entertain and the choices you make.

Your personal growth begins first, with your decision to take control of what you think, believe, and expect. Second, you must choose to make your thoughts and beliefs about yourself and life positive and constructive. Third, define your dream, believe in yourself, and surround yourself with people who also believe in you. Fourth, take the necessary steps outlined in this book to meet the challenges that will come your way. And finally, let yourself be guided by the universal laws of mind and spirit I have shared with you. Let them always be your guiding lights and your truest friends.

The best to you.

What You Can Do

A Quick Reference

This reference gives you quick access to ideas to help you in those areas that most concern you at any given time. These areas include family (Chapter 3), racism (Chapter 4), the need to overcome personal barriers (Chapter 5), and the challenges you face while taking charge of your life (Chapter 6). Just select the area of concern, then choose the wisdom that appeals to you most, and go directly to it.

Page

Chapter 3: Family

How to be strong for yourself whether your family life is supportive or nonsupportive.

1.	Get to know yours truly.	38
2.	Write your own scripts.	40
3.	Don't make your parents' problems your own.	40
4.	Try to understand.	39
5.	Let go.	39
6.	Do what you have to do and move on.	41
7.	Expand your playing field.	41
8.	Get jammin'. Focus on something worthwhile.	42
9.	Find and treasure your family's gifts for you.	42

Chapter 4: Racism

How to rise above racism and prevent it from getting the best of you.

1.	Turn the anger into something else.	49
2.	Cherish and celebrate your race.	50
3.	Don't hide from the beast.	51
4.	Mix it up!	51
5.	Look before you leap.	51
6.	Stay on your horse and ride.	52
7.	Educate yourself.	52

8.	Communicate effectively.	53
9.	Do the right thing - vote!	53
10.	Dismiss other people's negative stuff.	54
11.	Wish them growth.	54
12.	Don't look for racism.	55

Chapter 5: Overcoming Personal Barriers: Managing the Villain and the Hero Within

How to positively mange the forces of good and evil that are always present to influence and dominate your life.

1.	Confront the villain within.	61
2.	Embrace the hero and heroine within.	61
3.	Watch what you say to yourself.	61
4.	Don't' be a toy.	62
5.	Adopt a mentor.	63
6.	S-t-r-e-t-c-h yourself.	63
7.	Listen to the music.	64

Chapter 6: STRAIGHT UP: Taking Charge of Your Life

How to grow up feeling good and meet the challenges of moving into the world.

1.	Believe and invest in your magnificence.	73
2.	Broadcast your dreams.	73
3.	Keep your vehicle in good condition.	73
4.	Take good care of your self-esteem.	74
5.	Put together a tight crew.	79
6.	Don't be a gloom-and-doom junkie.	79
7.	Consider the source of the advice you get.	81
8.	Be a leader not a follower.	81
9.	Once more with emphasis:	81
	RESIST BELIEVING YOU ARE A VICTIM	81
10.	Face out.	82
11.	Pay your dues.	82
12.	Grow through your problems.	83
13.	Take Five	85
13.	Think and act like an entrepreneur.	85
14.	Move!	86

About the Author

Elizabeth Taylor-Gerdes, Ph.D.
Born May 1953, Chicago, Illinois.
Speaker, Educator, Thinker, and Consultant

Dr. Elizabeth Taylor-Gerdes is a recognized leader in the field of personal development, employment training, and motivation. She is the principal of Taylor-Gerdes Affiliates and Taylor/Gerdes Video in the San Francisco Bay Area. These are two firms that provide consulting, training, and video production services to a diverse clientele of public and private organizations.

Dr. Taylor-Gerdes earned a bachelor of science degree from the University of San Francisco, a master's degree in Human Resources and Organizational Development from the University of San Francisco, and a doctorate of Management and Organizational Development from the Union Institute, Cincinnati, Ohio. She has studied metaphysical sciences for 25 years.

For the past 15 years Dr. Taylor-Gerdes has taught college-level courses in industrial relations and urban studies, and helped corporate business leaders, nonprofits and public agencies address complex training and organizational development issues. She counsels and conducts workshops in self-esteem, personal management, employment and professional development, and spiritual growth. She has educated and motivated countless youths and adults to improve the quality of their personal and work lives.

Dr. Taylor-Gerdes lives with her husband and son. Among her favorite pastimes are reading, foreign films, world travel, horseback riding, theater, music, and comedy.